Angry with God

Angry with God

MICHELE NOVOTNI, PH.D. & RANDY PETERSEN

 PIÑON PRESS

P.O. Box 35007, Colorado Springs, CO 80935

OUR GUARANTEE TO YOU

We believe so strongly in the message of our books that we are making this quality guarantee to you. If for any reason you are disappointed with the content of this book, return the title page to us with your name and address and we will refund to you the list price of the book. To help us serve you better, please briefly describe why you were disappointed. Mail your refund request to: Piñon Press, P.O. Box 35007, Colorado Springs, CO 80935.

The Navigators is an international Christian organization. Our mission is to reach, disciple, and equip people to know Christ and to make Him known through successive generations. We envision multitudes of diverse people in the United States and every other nation who have a passionate love for Christ, live a lifestyle of sharing Christ's love, and multiply spiritual laborers among those without Christ.

NavPress is the publishing ministry of The Navigators. NavPress publications help believers learn biblical truth and apply what they learn to their lives and ministries. Our mission is to stimulate spiritual formation among our readers.

Cover design: Ray Moore
Cover art: PhotoSpin
Creative Team: Jacqueline Blakely, Terry Behimer, Glynese Northam

Unless otherwise identified, all Scripture quotations in this publication are taken from the *Holy Bible: New International Version*® (NIV). Copyright © 1973, 1978, 1984 by International Bible Society. Used by permission of Zondervan Publishing House. All rights reserved. Other versions used include: the *New American Standard Bible* (NASB), copyright © The Lockman Foundation 1960, 1962, 1963, 1968, 1971, 1972, 1973, 1975, 1977, 1995; the *New Revised Standard Version* (NRSV), copyright © 1989, by the Division of Christian Education of the National Council of the Churches of Christ in the USA, used by permission, all rights reserved; and the *King James Version* (KJV).

Novotni, Michele.
  Angry with God / Michele Novotni and Randy Petersen.
    p. cm.
  Includes bibliographical references.
  ISBN 1-57683-222-8 (pbk.)
    1. Anger--Religious aspects--Christianity. 2. Spiritual life--Christianity. I. Petersen, Randy. II. Title.

BV4627.A5 N68 2001
248.8'6--dc21

00-053030

Printed in the United States of America

1 2 3 4 5 6 7 8 9 10 / 05 04 03 02 01

FOR A FREE CATALOG OF
NAVPRESS BOOKS & BIBLE STUDIES,
CALL 1-800-366-7788 (USA)
OR 1-416-499-4615 (CANADA)

DEDICATION

This book is dedicated to the memory of

Helen Jamgochian.

We hope that telling your story will help

others—just as you desired.

CONTENTS

ACKNOWLEDGMENTS

We are indebted to all those who have opened their souls to us and shared their stories. To protect their privacy, we have changed names and minor details in the accounts of their experiences. However, we present Helen's story as precisely as we can, as she told it to Michele.

We specifically thank Harry Dorian, Esq., for his background information on the Armenian Genocide; Rev. Sturgis Poorman for his pastoral insights; Joanna Poorman for her manuscript review; Dr. Christopher Hall for his theological insights; and Dr. Freda Crews for her psychological and spiritual feedback. April Plassman provided reams of research as well as stories and insights, and we are deeply grateful. A number of professionals and students at Eastern College have been helpful in formulating this model, especially Bethany McDowell. Randy thanks the people of Hope United Methodist Church for their prayers.

Michele Novotni
Randy Petersen

INTRODUCTION

People who are hurting—who are sad, anxious, frustrated, or grieving—often struggle silently with their faith. Why must we suffer? Where is God in our suffering? Solid answers are hard to find. Some offer quick fixes that seem to raise more questions than they answer. The lack of answers can keep a sufferer locked in a state of frustration, or perhaps even full-blown anger at God.

And here's the most difficult part: many are afraid to give voice to this anger. Good people, we're told, don't ask questions. People of faith are supposed to trust God in all things. And so these unvoiced thoughts are often forced underground—pushed out of conscious thought, leaving people feeling disconnected from God but unable to do much about it.

The results are often troubling for those who do speak out in anger, as well. At times, well-meaning helpers can pile guilt or shame on any who dare to question God.

As a psychologist helping clients to work through their anger with people, I (Michele Novotni) noticed that there were parallels in their need to work through their anger with *God*. I saw working with anger as both a horizontal and vertical process. Unfortunately, I found few resources to help those who are angry at God. A book like this one seemed needed.

I was especially interested in this topic because of my grandmother Helen, whose questions raised the most important issues in poignant and deeply personal ways. For eight decades Helen stewed in anger against a God who, as she saw it, didn't help people in need. Helen was a survivor of the Armenian Genocide of 1915–1921, in which the Ottoman Turks killed more than 1.5 million Armenians and persecuted many more for their faith. In order to avoid persecution and death, one had only to denounce the Christian God and assume the Muslim faith. Those who clung to their faith were tortured or killed. The lucky ones were exiled.

As a child of twelve, Helen (her Armenian name was Armen) lost most of her family to the Turkish genocide. She couldn't help but wonder, *Where is God? How can God allow this to happen?* At the age of ninety-one, one week before she slipped into a coma and died, Helen finally made peace with God. She waited eighty years to let go of her anger with God and to experience his forgiveness.

In one of our last conversations, Helen said, "I'm an old woman. I'm going to die very soon. What can I do for my God now? I regret that I didn't make peace with God sooner. I regret that I didn't teach my children about God. All I can do now is let you tell others my story so that maybe they won't wait so long."

So this book is, in part, the story of Helen (Armen) Panosian Jamgochian, my grandmother, and her wrestling with God. This book is also a guide to help those who are hurting find their way to God. Helen had good reasons to be angry, and maybe you do too. We won't try to talk you out of anger, but we will talk you *through* it. And we'll keep offering the image of a compassionate God who keeps loving us, even when we have no clue what he's up to.

CHAPTER ONE

DARING TO ASK WHY

Helen awoke to the sound of her parents arguing in the living room. *Strange,* she thought, *they never fight.* The twelve year-old figured something big must be happening. Slipping out of bed, she crept to the top of the stairs. From her perch she could hear the argument.

"We must leave now," her mother was saying. "Things are getting too dangerous."

"And leave everything? They'll take it all, you know." Her father was a well-to-do merchant in town. He had built a profitable business and wasn't eager to give it up.

Young Helen heard her mother's sigh. "They will kill us. They're killing *all* the Christians."

"Then we'll lie. We'll just say we're Muslims. They'll let us be." There was a note of finality in her father's tone. He seemed to think that would be the end of it.

Helen's mother fought back tears. "How can you say that?" Although her husband shared her Christianity, he was not as devout as she. She was shocked that he could even imagine denying his faith.

"We'll just say the words," said Helen's father calmly. "In our hearts we will still worship God. God knows our hearts. He knows we have to do this."

"Say what you will," said Helen's mother. "I will never renounce my Jesus."

It was 1915. The Turks were taking over their region of Armenia, imposing their Muslim faith on Armenian Christians. Centuries of domination and harassment had exploded into violence. There were already reports of arrests and brutal murders in nearby towns. Now the Turks were threatening the Christians of Sivas, Helen's hometown. Her parents, Charlie and Anna Panosian, had been warned to convert, leave town, or die.

"Anna, be realistic," Charlie pled. "We have a good life here, I have a good position, we have a good home. What's wrong with wanting to keep all of this?"

Tucked away at the top of the stairs, Helen looked out at the exquisite Oriental carpets on the floor below, and the deft ironwork of the staircase that spiraled up to where she was sitting. She thought of her home's grand marble entryway, surrounded by lofty balconies. It was a house to be proud of, a place she enjoyed coming home to. But as her parents debated, Helen began to realize she might never see these things again.

"You do what you will," her mother said, "whatever you feel you must do. I am going to leave this country and take the children to safety."

Helen scurried back to bed, knowing her life would soon be changed forever. She didn't want to leave. She *liked* her life here — the marble entrance, the Oriental rugs, being waited on by servants. All this talk of Muslims and Christians seemed unimportant. Why couldn't they just leave her alone?

With all these worries, young Helen found it difficult to sleep, tossing and turning most of the night.

She was awakened before dawn. Apparently her mother had won the argument. Her entire family was fleeing — her father, too. Along with her younger brother and sisters, Helen was told to gather a few things and get ready to go. A few things? Dolls, toys, books, pictures, favorite clothes — there wasn't room for many of the things she loved. How can even a child pack her life in a small suitcase?

"This is just for a little while," she kept telling herself. "I'll be back. We'll all come back here." The more she said it, the more she knew it wasn't true. She had a sinking feeling in her heart that she would never see her home again.

An hour later, the Panosian family—Helen, her parents, and three younger siblings—stole out of their house, pushing a wheelbarrow piled high with suitcases. Her father carried his prayer beads; her mother held her Bible. As the sunrise cast an eerie glow, the streets of the neighborhood were shadowed by families leaving their homes, bundling their belongings and hurrying away.

Originally the Turks had promised to let the Armenians escape unharmed, but the policy changed suddenly. As they reached the border of the town, the Armenian families were stopped by Turkish troops.

Helen watched as her father was taken from them. In fact, all the men in the group were taken from their families. The women and children were placed in a large circle surrounding an inner cluster of Armenian men. Soldiers would grab one man at a time and ask, "Will you renounce your God?" If the man said no, they shot him in the head. But if the Christian renounced his faith, he was allowed to join his family along the outer circle.

Many brave Armenian men refused to save their lives by renouncing their faith. Would Helen's father be one of them? The girl watched in horror as the Turkish soldiers methodically approached each man. She averted her eyes as shot after shot pierced the morning air. The street was now paved with bloody bodies, but Helen's eyes focused on her father, standing stiffly in the cold, clutching his string of prayer beads. She remembered his voice from the night before: *Just say the words. God knows our hearts.* She hoped he would have the sense to do this. How would the family ever get along without him? How would she ever get along without him? *Just say the words!*

They pulled him forward. Helen heard her mother gasp behind

her. They barked out the question: "Will you renounce your Christian God?"

He paused.

What was going through her father's mind at that moment? Helen always wondered that. Was he weighing his obligation to his family against his loyalty to God? Was he inspired by the courage of his fallen brothers? What prayers was he praying as he clutched the prayer beads?

"Just say the words!" his eldest daughter was screaming, amid the shrieks and wails of the crowd. "We need you!"

"No," her father said, looking lovingly at his family with tears in his eyes. "I cannot renounce my God."

The gun went off. He fell. Her mother screamed. And a door slammed shut in Helen's heart.

When the carnage was done, Helen's mother rushed to her husband's dead body. Weeping, she gathered the prayer beads from his hand.

Facing the Questions

Helen was my grandmother. I knew her many years later, of course, and she was still holding a grudge against God. It would take her eighty years to move beyond her anger with God. Unfortunately, that day in 1915, when her father was killed for refusing to renounce his faith, was just the beginning of her trials. We'll be telling more of her story throughout this book.

Many people feel it is wrong to be angry with God, and they repress these feelings within themselves. But when they hear a story like Helen's, even they find it difficult to fault her. Certainly she had more than her share of pain and suffering—many reasons to be mad at God. Yet by looking at her troubles, and her understandable emotional responses to those troubles, maybe we can gain insight into our own experiences and emotions.

You don't need to survive a genocide in order to be angry with God. There are plenty of valid reasons, and we will discuss them. As we trace Helen's emotional and spiritual journey toward peace, we hope that you may find hope and help for your situation as well.

The Armenian Genocide was brutal, an episode of gross inhumanity in which the Muslims in power sought to exterminate the Christian Armenians. This was not an isolated event, however. Throughout history, many nations have attempted their own versions of "ethnic cleansing." Helen's story involves Muslims persecuting Christians, but those who claim the name of Christ have been guilty of atrocities too.

Suffering isn't limited to these large-scale patterns of violence, of course. People also suffer from everyday losses and struggles. Loved ones die. We become ill. Prayers don't seem to be answered. People become overwhelmed, frustrated, or depressed with the weight of living. Questions often surface—*Where is God? Does God really care about any of us? How can God let this happen?*

It often seems to the victims of such tragedies that God either is ignoring us or is powerless to help us. Either God doesn't care or God doesn't matter.

Philosophers have wrestled with "the problem of evil" for centuries, and we'll let them continue to do so. These are tough questions, and this book isn't focused on philosophy. But we do offer help and hope from a *psychological* perspective for those who are struggling.

Because I (Michele) am a psychologist, I often counsel people who have gone through difficult experiences. As a result, many of them do what my grandmother did—they rail against God either inwardly or outwardly. They hold grudges. They get angry. *If you're going to be like that, God, then I just won't believe in you anymore!* Sometimes people don't even know that they are angry at God. Sometimes they know, but are afraid to think, let alone utter, such a thought.

This book is about healing and reconciliation, about giving voice to those spoken or unspoken questions. How do you go from breaking up to making up? How do you make peace with a God who remains silent? How do you make peace with a God who seems to have declared war on you?

The Stages of Grief

Sharon came for counseling during an exceptionally painful time of her life. Within six months, she had lost both her mother and her grandmother to illness. And then her two daughters were suddenly killed in a car accident. Grieving is tough enough when one person we love dies. But to lose four loved ones in such a short time — we can hardly blame Sharon for questioning God's purposes.

Grief over the loss of loved ones follows natural patterns. Elisabeth Kübler-Ross and others have written extensively about the stages of human grieving. We *deny* first, then we get *angry.* Then there's usually a time of *bargaining,* when we try to make things better. A period of *depression* then precedes the point of *acceptance.* This is a general progression, but it's not clockwork — emotions are not linear. People can bounce around a bit in the years following a tragedy, slipping back to anger or even denial. But generally there is progressive movement through these stages, and eventually a person reaches a place of acceptance.

Some folks talk about "getting over" their grief. But healthy people don't get over it — they go *through* it. Successful grieving doesn't shut out pain; it accepts the suffering and moves on.

Problems occur when people get stuck in the grieving process. Perhaps they linger too long in denial. Parents might keep the room of a dead son just as it was when he was alive — as if he were still there. That's normal for a while, but if it remains there for years, that's an indication that something is wrong. Other people lock into anger. Tragedy turns them bitter, and their attitude can remain toxic for the rest of their lives.

As Sharon tried to deal with the multiple deaths in her family, she was in danger of getting stuck between denial and anger. "I believe God loves me," she said, "and he must have a plan for all this, but I sure don't know what it is." Friends from her church tried to be helpful by sugarcoating her loss. They assured her that she'd see these four dear departed souls in heaven someday, and so she should look forward to that day. They reminded her that her loved ones were in a better place, and that she should be happy for them. Some suggested that these events would build her character, so she should rejoice rather than mourn.

All in all, the message she received from her friends was: "Don't grieve." She learned to hide her tears from others. Any display of grief would only bring another well-intentioned lecture. She was getting stuck in denial. Oh, she wasn't denying that her mother, grandmother, and daughters had died, but she was being urged to deny her own sadness. She was not "supposed to" feel bad about it, and so she tried not to. Telling herself that God had her best interests in mind, she tried to go about her life with a positive outlook.

But as she talked, it became evident that Sharon was filled with a quiet anger. Somewhere inside her, she needed to move on to the next stage of grieving, and her anger was simmering. But who would she be angry at? Could she be mad at her mother for dying? How could she rant at her daughters for being in an accident? Maybe she could rage against the other driver or the disease that took her grandmother, but the collection of deaths in her family—so many in such a short time—was pointing to one culprit, someone she dare not blame: God.

That seems wrong, doesn't it? Even if you know nothing else about God, you know he's supposed to be holy, just, and good. "God is great and God is good," you may have prayed over your peanut butter sandwiches. God is the *definition* of goodness. So how can people even imagine that God has wronged them?

That was Sharon's problem. She believed that God loved her, but after that horrendous six-month period, she didn't *feel* very loved. She had been knocked down by tragedy and then kicked when she was down, and then kicked again. It wasn't fair! But because she believed in God's goodness, she had to figure that these bad things were somehow good, that God had sent these calamities for her benefit. But then why did she feel so bad? Why was she suffering so much? And how could she even think about questioning God? What was wrong with her?

The grieving process can derail early when we won't let ourselves become angry at God. We tell ourselves, "God must be using this misfortune for some good purpose, so I shouldn't feel so bad about it. I must not feel this pain I'm feeling." That's denial. In order for the grieving process to continue in a healthy way, a sufferer needs to acknowledge his or her feelings—even the ugly feelings. Sharon needed to say, "God has been unfair to me!" In fact, she needed to pound on heaven's door and wail, "My God, why have you forsaken me?" She wouldn't be the first; both the psalmist and Jesus used those words.

It takes that kind of honesty to break the logjam of denial and allow the grieving process to continue.

Let's take a moment to assure the faithful that we're not trying to question God's goodness. But Sharon's crisis in that moment was emotional, not theological. From a psychological perspective, Sharon needed to be encouraged to *feel her feelings,* to admit her anger, even if it might prove later to be unfounded.

Honesty is the best policy, especially with God. Some people who are scrupulously honest in their human relationships still have trouble being completely open when they pray. Ken Taylor, an administrator at Taylor University, tells a story of his young son who complained loudly about what the family was having for dinner one night. To make a point, Ken asked the boy to say the prayer over the meal. "Dear God," the youngster said sweetly, "thank you for helping us this day at school, thank you for our family, and thank you for the wonderful meal that Mom has made. Amen." After the prayer, Ken announced that he thought God was sick to his stomach, because God wants people to share their honest thoughts and feelings with him. What his son should have prayed, Ken suggested, was "Dear God, you know I don't like what Mom has cooked tonight, but help me to be able to eat enough so my parents will not be upset with me!"

To hide your true feelings in the interest of theological correctness is downright unhealthy. And futile. After all, doesn't God know our hearts? He doesn't need to hear the words to know what we are thinking and feeling. We don't need to be polite with him. If we're upset, he knows it. We only hurt ourselves by bottling up those feelings.

Many people have a hard time expressing anger toward anyone. In our polite society, we're supposed to smile all the time. We mustn't get angry with our children, our coworkers, or our spouses. That's the accepted wisdom, but it's wrong! Only through honestly wrestling with where you are emotionally can you move on.

What Is Anger?

Let's talk about anger. What is it?

In the field of counseling, anger is a signal, and one worth listening to. In the words of Harriet Lerner, "Our anger may be a message that we are being hurt, that our rights are being violated, that our needs or wants are not being adequately met, or simply that something is not right."[1] In the best cases, anger supplies the energy to set things right. Many great reformers throughout history were fueled by anger at the way things were, and they set about to change them.

But anger isn't precise. It's a fire that burns anything in its path. Fire is great for heating food and roasting marshmallows, but it can also burn down houses and forests. Anger often lashes out at inappropriate targets. This is called *displacement,* and it looks something like this:

> A man is treated badly by his boss and goes home
> to yell at his wife.

> The woman is hurt by her husband, so she yells at
> her kids.

> The children are angered by their parents, so they
> pick fights with other children.

And round and round it goes.

This lack of precision sometimes makes it hard to figure out the real cause of our anger. We pile up offenses and rage against them all, scorching everyone in our path. It's no wonder that many are afraid of this unharnessed emotion. Or maybe the anger goes underground and we nurse grudges, developing a general bitterness. This kind of repressed anger often goes unnoticed for a long time.

Anger has sometimes been defined as "a natural response to a perceived threat." Anthropologists might hark back to prehistoric times when a cave dweller needed an adrenaline rush to beat back the saber-toothed tiger at the door. But true anger is deeper than that. It deals not only with threats, but also with *injustice.* We respond angrily when we feel someone is being victimized—especially when *we're* the ones being treated unfairly.

There's a stoplight near my (Randy's) home that always seems to turn red as I approach it. That makes me mad. I'm not sure who or what I'm angry *at,* but I feel unfairly singled out, as if the traffic planners programmed the stoplight specifically to hinder my progress. That's ridiculous, of course, but that doesn't matter. What matters is that, in that moment, I feel as if I am the victim of an unjust traffic plot.

Here's another example. I went to see a play recently and found that my assigned seat was taken. The lights were already dimming, so rather than making a scene, I slipped into another seat across the aisle. But throughout the play, I was distracted by the man who was sitting in *my* seat. The man kept fidgeting, clearing his throat, laughing at the wrong times. "How ignorant!" I thought, my self-righteous anger brewing. "Some people just don't know how to behave in public."

But when the lights came up at intermission, I got a closer look. The man seemed to be limited in some way. From the way he was treated by the friends around him, I surmised that he might have a developmental disability. And that would explain the erratic movements during the play, the inappropriate laughter, and so on. The man really *didn't* know how to behave in public, but that wasn't his fault. Suddenly my attitude softened, the anger melted away. Wasn't it great that this man was brought to see a play? What a growing experience for this struggling soul!

What had changed? Nothing, really. In the second act, the man was still sitting in the wrong seat, still distracting others—but now there was no anger. Why? The threat to my viewing pleasure was the same, but now my perception of the *justice* of the situation was entirely different. Because the man had his own problems to deal with, I was willing to excuse the distracting behavior.

Usually you don't have that much time to analyze situations. Something happens and you make a snap judgment, fueling your feelings of anger. You might then express those feelings in angry words or actions, or hold them back and store them inside. In some cases, as with the man in the theater, the feelings can be reevaluated and transformed.

But that's the pattern of anger:

1. Some problematic situation occurs;
2. you perceive injustice in it;
3. your natural emotions well up; and
4. you react, inwardly or outwardly.

Anger is an emotional event, and it needs to run its course. We're not saying that anger always has to result in a verbal or physical outburst, but it needs to go *somewhere.* It's like starting up a computer. Push the button, and the machine starts whirring into action, going through its startup ritual. But let's say you change your mind and decide not to use the computer. You could just pull the plug or push the on/off button, but that's not good for the computer. You're supposed to go through a designated shut-down routine so the computer can go through its closing rituals and turn off in a healthy manner.

Anger is just like that. Once it starts up, it may take a while for it to shut down. This is true even if you learn that your perception was wrong. That is, even if you realize that the situation that sparked your anger doesn't really exist, you have still "started up" your angry response. You need to go through a "shut-down" process.

Many people try to deny their anger—all anger, not just anger directed at God. They feel uncomfortable with their angry feelings, maybe even afraid of them, so they pretend the feelings aren't there. But that doesn't change the fact that the angry feelings have started up—*something* must be done with them. Sheila Carney writes,

> Denying feelings of anger doesn't eliminate them. It simply pushes them into our unconscious where they are alive, active and seeking expression. Because we

lose control over the things we suppress, we are no longer able to understand or evaluate them.[2]

That's the danger of denying our anger toward God. Though we may pretend that everything's fine, the suppressed anger becomes a kind of cancer, eating away at us, *even if we don't realize it.* We lose control of our feelings when we send them underground. They can create a general bitterness that poisons our attitudes even when we have stopped thinking about the initial cause of those negative feelings.

Anger's Options

So, once we perceive injustice and respond emotionally to it—that is, once we feel anger—what should we do? We have several options, all somewhat dangerous. We can express our anger, but that can often get us in big trouble. Temper tantrums can harm marriages, alienate our friends, and cause us to lose our jobs. The imprecise nature of anger means that we may end up treating others unfairly, and they may respond with anger toward us.

For this reason, many of us have learned not to express anger. When we're upset, we "count to ten," which isn't such a bad idea—except that many of us just keep on counting and never express our feelings at all. Carol Christ writes, "Those of us who grew up in a white middle class culture have been taught that anger is not 'nice' and have learned to suppress our anger so successfully that often we have hidden it even from ourselves."[3] But that's not only true of "white middle class culture." People of some subcultures seem to be pretty free in expressing their anger, but many others aren't. The point is that broad groups of us have been taught that expressing our anger is dangerous.

But if expressing anger is dangerous, so is stuffing it. As we've just said, that fire can burn within us for years, charring our own souls. In counseling, I (Michele) have seen marriages falling apart from dry rot. The partners are very civil to each other, but they harbor deep resentments. One of the best things I can do for such couples is to help them express their feelings—especially the anger, hurt, and disappointment.

If they can learn to express their resentment without demolishing the other person's spirit, there's hope for the relationship. We need to find a middle path: expression without destruction. Let the fire burn a little without consuming everything in sight.

With all the difficulty we have in expressing anger toward other people, it's not surprising that people have trouble expressing their anger toward God. If it's not "nice" to bark at your spouse, it has to be some major transgression to rail against your heavenly Father. Yell at your neighbor, and he might take a swing at you; yell at God, and who knows what lightning bolts might come your way?

Therefore, many are afraid even to admit their feelings of anger when God is the object. They don't just fail to express these feelings, they shut down those emotions entirely. And just as repressed anger may result in a passionless marriage or a shallow friendship, it can also keep one's relationship with God from being all it can be.

Back in 1951, Aaron Rutledge observed this phenomenon:

> To many emotionally upset Christians the mere mention of prayer or of religion is sufficient to send them into an anxiety attack, for they are afraid of God. Others . . . have departed active church life because of frustration in the attempt to find help there, and bitterness against the day they professed faith is not unusual. "My fellow Christians let me down; the church let me down; God let me down"—and now having rebelled, they feel God is stalking them in a vindictive mood.[4]

Despair and serious discouragement might best be thought of as quiet rebellion. People are afraid to raise their voices against heaven. Instead, they sink into frustration, bitterness, and anxiety, withdrawing from the community of faith and drifting away from any meaningful relationship with God.

So when you feel wronged by God and the anger starts welling up, how should you respond? Or if you have a friend with those feelings, what should you say? Let's consider some of the common approaches.

"It's Wrong to Be Angry at God"

Many people assume this, and it sounds logical. We think of anger as something that makes enemies, and we don't want to be God's enemy. But let's take a closer look at this idea.

If anger is a natural response to a perceived injustice, then there are at least two good things about it. First, God gave it to us. He hardwired this anger response into our emotions. That doesn't mean that every expression of anger is holy, but it does mean that God understands our feelings.

The second good thing about anger is that it promotes justice—at least it's supposed to. Anger is based on a desire to be treated fairly and to see others treated fairly. Our perception of justice is often skewed, but ideally anger is a way God has given us to signal that something is going wrong.

But when we're angry at God, does that mean we're accusing him of doing wrong? Are we saying that he is unjust? Yes and no. We're saying that we *feel* he is treating us unfairly. As long as we understand that we could be mistaken about this, we should be able to express our feelings. Those feelings can *still* be a signal that something is going wrong in our relationship with God but we'll never find out what is wrong if we never say how we feel.

Perhaps the strongest testimony to the validity of expressing anger toward God is the all-star lineup of people who have done so. The Judeo-Christian tradition is rich with people who argued freely with their Lord. Abraham, Moses, Samuel, David, Elijah, Job, Jeremiah, Peter, and Paul all expressed anger, frustration, disagreement, or disappointment in their relationship with God. In a few cases they were corrected, but generally their honesty seemed to draw them into a closer relationship with God.

When we insist that it's wrong to be angry at God, we don't stop the anger—we just stuff it deeper, where it will probably do more damage. And we add a huge dose of guilt. So not only are people upset about being treated unfairly by God, they also feel frustrated about their inability to do anything about it. Some feel that they must be very wicked people because they have those feelings. How could God ever love them when they have such sinful emotions?

The "it's-wrong-to-be-angry-with-God" approach is unhelpful and potentially damaging. It's best to reserve judgment on our anger until we understand the purpose and potential of anger in healing relationships—even relationships with God.

"There Is No Good Reason to Be Angry at God—He's Perfect"

At a workshop, Michele heard one participant sum up this response well: "There isn't any use getting mad at God. God is always right, so I must be wrong. I'll just have to get over it. After all, God is God."

This gets to the crux of the logic of our anger. If we feel God is treating us unfairly, we must be wrong, because God is perfectly holy and just. Therefore, it makes no sense to be angry at God.

That sounds right, but anger is seldom so logical. We *feel* angry based on our *perceptions* of justice, often before we have a chance to reason things out fully.

Let's say a woman comes home an hour late from work on the day her husband was planning to take her out for their anniversary. He's been sitting at home stewing, getting angrier by the minute, unaware that she's delayed by a huge traffic tie-up. When she comes home, he lets her have it: "Don't you know what day this is? Isn't our anniversary important to you? How could you be so inconsiderate?" But then she explains about the traffic, reaffirms her love for him, and apologizes. His anger subsides.

Note that it *subsides* — it doesn't vanish. His emotion has gotten his heart rate going, his blood pressure up, and his palms sweating. These physiological responses will take a few minutes to return to normal, as he mutters an apology and calls the restaurant to change the reservation. He may even redirect his anger away from his wife and toward, say, the Department of Transportation for doing road construction during rush hour.

Now let's imagine that this husband doesn't express his anger, but instead keeps it inside. His wife comes home and he greets her "kindly" and "calmly" as he calls the restaurant, all the while nursing a grudge. He never complains, so she never explains. His perception of the situation is that his wife didn't care about their anniversary dinner, and he'll keep holding that perception as he continues to stuff his anger.

Remember: once the process of anger begins, that anger has to go somewhere. It may be defused, diffused, or deflated, or redirected to some other object. Or we may stuff it inside ourselves. Communication allows us to do something healthy with our anger. It may get us to change the perception that made us angry in the first place. That's true not only in our interpersonal relationships, but also in our relationship with God. Only by communicating with him — complaining, maybe, but also listening — can we begin to understand his perfect justice.

We have to admit that God may *seem* unfair in his dealings with us. We can trust that his plans will ultimately work out for our good, but often it's hard to see where it's all leading. Maybe if we had perfect faith we would always see the future blessings in our present problems, but we don't. And we're not alone. Our lineup of biblical heroes joins us in questioning God's actions. "Why, O LORD, do you stand far off? Why do you hide yourself in times of trouble?" asks the psalmist (Psalm 10:1). "Why do you hide your face and forget our misery and oppression?" (Psalm 44:24). In several of the Psalms, the author wonders why God allows the wicked to prosper while the righteous suffer.

So there's no shame in asking the questions. You're allowed to tell God how you feel. Be honest about how things look from your vantage point—even if you suspect that God's viewpoint is different. God's ways are beyond our ways; his wisdom is often hidden from us. Our emotions are based on our limited percep-tions, and we don't always understand what God is doing. But we still feel our feelings, and we have to do something with those feelings. It's best to express them honestly.

"How Can You Love God and Be Angry at Him at the Same Time?"

This question assumes that love and anger can't coexist, and it's based on a faulty understanding of both. Love is far more than a collection of positive feelings toward someone. It's a commitment to make that person important in your life. And anger is not nec-essarily a rejection of someone. As we've said, it's a signal that something is wrong.

If someone is important to you, you want to recognize when something is wrong and see what you can do to make it right. If someone you don't know bumps into you at the mall, you might feel a flash of anger, but you don't need to do much about it. There's no relationship there. But if someone you love makes you mad, you have to deal with it. Love creates a relationship that you want to nurture, and that makes it worth the risk of expressing your feelings, including anger.

In some troubled marriages, the couples simply don't care enough anymore to talk about their conflicts. They've put on emotional armor, which keeps them from fighting but also keeps them from loving. The same thing can happen in your relationship with God. When you fail to express your anger, you're limiting the emotional depth of your relationship. In a way, you're giving up on God, assuming that he doesn't care how you really feel.

William Gaultiere wrote about the biblical character of Job, the sufferer. God allowed some terrible things to happen to this man, and then Job and his philosopher friends spent thirty chapters trying to assign blame. "Despite [Job's] tremendous emotional suffering and God's apparent absence in the midst of his pain, he did not give up on God. He loved and trusted God so much that he had the guts to be emotionally honest with God and tell Him he felt angry and hateful toward Him for apparently being so unfair and mean to Him."[5]

It's amazing how people try to protect God, as if he'll be emotionally damaged if they say anything negative to him. God's love is strong enough to withstand our emotions; after all, he's the one who created them. The Bible shows us a God who debates, teases, teaches, and even wrestles with people. If we truly want a love relationship with God, we won't try to "protect" him from our true feelings. We'll tell him how we feel and then see what happens.

"Let's Get the Issues on the Table and Sort Through Them"

This is the approach we're proposing. It works with human relationships and it's the best option when you've got issues with God. Grudges do great damage. When you hold your anger within, unexpressed, it eats away at you and stunts the growth of your relationships. Only by opening up can you move forward. Only then can you discuss what makes you angry, evaluate your perception of the situation, and maybe correct the problem.

It's always risky to express your honest feelings. In human relationships, you can be misunderstood. Your anger can spark anger in the other person. Or you may realize that your feelings are ill-founded. You may end up embarrassed at the fact that your righteous anger isn't so righteous after all.

Some of the same risks apply when you express anger to God, but it's worth it. Gaultiere writes,

> Misunderstanding, disagreement, and conflict are inevitable in any relationship, especially one in which a sinful human being tries to relate to an invisible God in a fallen world. Thus, if we want to have an honest and intimate relationship with God we need to be willing to "wrestle with God.". . . Among the Christians I work with in therapy, it has been my experience that those who are willing to honestly wrestle with God by confronting, questioning, or even complaining to Him about the pain and injustice they experience are the ones who develop the most intimate relationship with Him.[6]

You might be familiar with the poem "Footprints":

> *One night a man dreamed he was walking*
> *Along the beach with the Lord.*
> *As scenes of his life flashed before him,*
> *He noticed that there were two sets of footprints*
> *in the sand. He also noticed*
> *At his saddest, lowest times there was but one*
> *Set of footprints. This bothered the man.*

He asked the Lord, "Did you not promise that if
I gave my heart to you
That you'd be with me all the way?
Then why is there but one set of footprints
During my most troublesome times?"
The Lord replied, "My precious child, I love you
And would never forsake you.
During those times of trial and suffering,
When you see only one set of footprints,
It was then I carried you."

This anonymous poem is widely known as an inspirational expression of deep devotion. But did you see the anger? Right there in the middle is a complaint: "Didn't you promise this? Why only one set of footprints?" In other words, "Where were you when I needed you, God?" Imagine how this story would go if this anger were never expressed. Let's say this poet sought counseling from a friend who said, "Oh, no, you mustn't be angry at God." Would the poet deny his or her true feelings? "Maybe there really were two sets of footprints the whole time." Or maybe the poet would just stuff those emotions, feeling betrayed by God but never saying so.

The victory of this poem is its honesty. The poet dares to challenge the Lord, and the Lord responds. Maybe you'll never get such a clear response to your questions, but you'll never know unless you ask.

CHAPTER TWO

WHY DO BAD THINGS HAPPEN?

Twelve-year-old Helen didn't have much of a chance to mourn the execution of her father. More suffering awaited her. Her family, like many Armenian families in Turkey during 1915, would be torn apart and brutalized.

Helen's father died clutching prayer beads, refusing to renounce his Christian faith, just one of a number of Armenian men herded together and killed as their families looked on. The same scene played out in other Armenian towns: the knock on the door, the hasty gathering of possessions, the mass exodus halted, the men massacred, the women and children herded along. Like other attempts throughout history to wipe out a particular race or faith, the Turkish efforts had a chilling efficiency. This was no crime of passion by a few hotheaded murderers letting their nationalistic zeal take hold. No, these atrocities were *planned*.

The Ottoman Turks had dominated the Armenians for centuries. The Armenians, who were largely Christian, were accustomed to being second-class citizens in Muslim Turkey, but the late 1800s saw an escalation of the violence against them. One sultan slaughtered hundreds of thousands of Armenians in the 1890s, but a group called the Young Turks came to power in the new century, promising democratic reforms. Armenian hopes for greater freedom were soon dashed as the new rulers launched a methodical genocide against them. There had been approximately

2.5 million Armenians in Turkey before 1915; the genocide reportedly wiped out 1.5 million of them.

First, the leaders of Armenian society were killed. It happened in many towns just as it happened in Sivas, Helen's town—the heads of the households were rounded up and murdered as their families were forced to watch. Then the young men of Armenia were drafted into the army but given no weapons. During World War I these Armenian soldiers were used as cannon fodder or killed for deserting. Finally, most of the women and children were rounded up and "relocated"—forced to march across the desert to some new "home" that most would never reach. Some of these Armenian Christians could save themselves by recanting their faith and assimilating into the Turkish Muslim culture. Some did, but many others, like Helen's parents, refused.

Even now it's troubling to note the veneer of legality on these proceedings. The Turkish authorities were trumping up charges— spying, treason, desertion—and then executing the Armenians for their "crimes." They were "merely" taxing or drafting or relocating the Armenian people. This kept the international community quiet. Besides, the world had a war to worry about. (Germany, which was allied with Turkey in World War I, learned from the Turks' methods and later applied some of them against the Jews.)

Helen's eight-year-old brother, Haroutune, was taken away and put in a house with many other young Armenian boys and men. Kerosene was poured throughout the building and the doors and windows were boarded and nailed shut. Then the house was set afire.

Mothers and sisters looked on as the flames raged, hearing screams from inside the house. Turkish soldiers guarded the property, taunting the helpless onlookers. "Is your God not powerful enough to make a cloud of rain come to put out this little fire we made? How mighty is your God if he can't put out a little fire? Maybe he doesn't have the power. Or if he does, he must not care for you very much. Why won't he put out the fire? How could a loving God let all these children die? Here you all are, praying to your God. Why doesn't he hear your prayers?"

Their taunting stuck in young Helen's mind. These were the questions she'd been thinking about since the death of her father, although she hadn't yet put them into words. In contrast, her mother remained a rock of faith, accepting these horrific events and continuing to pray and praise God. But Helen became angrier and angrier. "How can you pray to this God who lets your son burn up, who allows your husband to die in his name?" she asked her mother. "If God is real, how can he let these awful things happen to us?"

The Problem of Evil

It's hard to blame Helen for feeling that way. The Turkish officers posed the dilemma perfectly: either God doesn't have the power to help us or he doesn't truly love us. That, in a nutshell, is the "problem of evil" that philosophers have wrestled with for ages. How can evil exist in a world overseen by an all-loving, all-powerful God? If he truly had both of those qualities, the argument goes, he would spare us this pain.

We could understand a God who was loving but weak. In fact, certain modern theologians have gone in that direction. God cares deeply for us, they say, but there's only so much he can do.

We could understand a God who was all-powerful but didn't care about us. We wouldn't like that, but we'd understand it. He oversees everything, but in a strange, whimsical way—so goes that notion. But is there no justice? Even if we give up the idea of a loving God, we still want a God who plays fair. And what did the Armenians do to deserve genocide? Or the Jews? Or the Kosovars? And what did a grieving parent do to deserve the death of a child, or a wife the loss of her husband, or a youth an injury that paralyzes him?

Emotional Atheism

Some find it easier not to believe in God at all. That was young Helen's decision. In counterpoint to her mother's enduring belief, Helen chose disbelief. As the atrocities mounted, she knew only two things: there was no God, and she was very angry at him.

You can see the absurdity of these two notions. How can you be mad at someone who doesn't exist? But that's how Helen felt for most of her life, and many others feel the same way, even if they don't state it quite so obviously. Early in his life, the noted Christian writer C. S. Lewis was a bitter unbeliever. "I maintained that God did not exist," he wrote later. "I was also very angry with God for not existing."[1]

Anger inspires revenge, but how can you get back at God? If you blame God for the evils he has allowed, what can you possibly do to punish him? Stop believing in him. That'll teach him.

Seriously, that's the route many people take, consciously or unconsciously. They shut God out of their lives because that's the only thing they can do to protest his actions (or his inaction). It may be many years before they let him back in, if they ever do.

Granted, some choose atheism because they feel that's the most sensible answer to the problem of evil. Atrocities happen, they conclude, because there is no governing force in the universe to prevent atrocities from happening. This is an intellectual decision, not an emotional one, and so it's really outside the scope of this book. We're talking about people who are angry at God, people who let that passion propel them into an *emotional atheism*. Their intellectual conclusions are reached through their emotional response to perceived injustice.

When Miriam was seventeen, she decided there was no God. There was a school bus accident in her neighborhood and little children were killed. How could God allow such a tragedy? Though she was brought up in a Jewish home and taught about God, she made her own choice at that moment to stop believing.

For the next twenty-five years, she considered herself an atheist—not because she had examined the evidence for and against God's existence, but because of this one event. She just couldn't believe in a God who let school buses run over innocent children. After a while, the emotion of that event subsided, but her conclusion remained. It's a bit like losing touch with a distant relative: once he's out of your life, it's just easier to keep him out.

In her forties, Miriam developed a good friendship with Rae Ann, a woman who had a passionate belief in God. They talked about everything, including God. While Rae Ann never tried to foist her faith upon Miriam, it was infectious. One day, Miriam said, "You know, I stopped believing in God when I was seventeen." It was a moment of self-discovery for her, as if she had unearthed some buried clue, and the story came out. The school bus. The children. That's why she stopped believing. It all seemed so definitive at the time. And she just had no reason to change her mind, until now. Rae Ann's faith had forced Miriam to reevaluate her decision.

That's how it goes for many who choose emotional atheism. It's more of a passionate decision than an intellectual one. Yet they may not reconsider the issue until decades later, when the original passion is long past.

One of my (Michele's) clients, Linda, entered counseling without a belief in God. She adamantly explained that she wasn't interested in any form of Christian counseling, but she did want help with her life situation. Then she told her story of growing up too soon, without having a chance to experience a real childhood.

Linda was an only child and both of her parents were very ill when she was little. Since they lived in an isolated area, she found herself caring for two ailing parents, essentially running the household. This was her life from about the age of five: toiling from sunup to sundown.

Her mother, a very devout Christian, prayed constantly. She clung to her faith as her health failed. Linda heard her prayers, but saw no response from God. She too prayed for her parents' healing, but both became sicker and eventually died. She was left alone. From that point on she decided that God wasn't there. It would be many years before Linda reevaluated her decision.

Anger at God can be strong enough to last a lifetime—especially unexamined anger. We want people to be clear on the reasons behind that rejection. Do you choose not to believe in God because the world makes more sense without him? Or because he has hurt you?

Obviously, Linda was dealing with deep emotional issues. Intellectually, she had decided the best reason for the unanswered prayers of her family was that there was no God to answer them. That's an option, of course, but not the only one. There are many reasons to believe in God, even when we don't understand his actions. When you consider all the evidence, it often takes more of a leap of faith to be an atheist than to believe in God. If you feel you've made an intellectual choice to reject belief in God, we encourage you to take another look at the issue.

We also believe there are many reasons to be angry at God. And there are many possible outlets for that anger, but disbelief is a short-sighted choice. In Linda's case, the problems were primarily emotional, not intellectual. Yet, in her youth, she grabbed an intellectual way to get back at the God she blamed for her emotional pain—she denied his existence.

That's an understandable choice in the heartache of the moment, but it's not the best long-term position. That intellectual solution doesn't really solve the emotional problem, because the sufferer is blocking out the existence of the God who can offer help and healing.

So allow yourself to be angry. Express that anger. But don't walk away from the relationship that can help you.

The Problem Solvers

And watch out for the problem solvers, those who have a Bible passage or platitude ready for every occasion.

They mean well, most of them, but they're liable to fill you with shame and guilt, which can make you even *more* angry. Their favorite weapon is a beautiful Bible verse from one of the apostle Paul's letters: "All things work together for good" (Romans 8:28, KJV). Nothing wrong with the verse itself; it's just that the problem solvers can wield it in an insensitive and ill-timed way.

"No need to feel bad," they say, "because all things work together for good."

"If you had faith, you wouldn't be so upset," they say. "Don't you believe that all things work together for good?"

"God has a plan," they say, "so don't you worry your little head about that problem. Just wait and see how he's going to work it all out for good."

"Praise the Lord for that atrocity!" they say. "He's going to work it all out."

The problem isn't so much in *what* they say, but in *how* and *when* they say it. It's not outrageous to suggest that there might be some divine stratagem involved in the events that torment us. But these facile comments minimize everything—the events, the horror, and your pain. They can trigger your sense of guilt or shame for feeling a natural repulsion against terrible things that happen. To say, essentially, "Don't worry, be happy," in the face of the Armenian Genocide or Nazi concentration camps is not faith but emotional anesthesia.

Such events shake us. They *must* shake us, if we're paying attention at all. We are forced to ask the hard questions, such as "Where is God when all this is happening?" And of course our suffering doesn't need to be the result of genocide to elicit feelings of hurt, disappointment, or anger with God.

We're not alone in our questions. One part of the Bible that the problem solvers tend to ignore is a batch of Psalms that cry out in this same way:

> *My tears have been my food day and night,*
> *while men say to me all day long,*
> *"Where is your God?"...*
> *I say to God my Rock,*
> *"Why have you forgotten me?*
> *Why must I go about mourning,*
> *oppressed by the enemy?"*
> *My bones suffer mortal agony*
> *as my foes taunt me,*
> *saying to me all day long,*
> *"Where is your God?"*
> (Psalm 42:3,9-10)

To cry out to God in the face of injustice and human misery is not a *lack* of faith. It is the very *essence* of faith. We cannot bury the hard questions under the topsoil of too-easy Bible texts. We must take these hard questions to the only one who can possibly answer them.

Later, a time may come when we can understand our tears. But right now, in our emotional and spiritual understanding, we are where we are. We feel what we feel. And we need people to sit with us in our sorrow and grief—not try to fix it, not try to make it all better. We need to be met where we are so that we can journey where we need to go. Romans 8:28 will provide strength, hope, and encouragement—but that's probably a little farther down the road.

Back to the Problem

The problem solvers are often compassionate people, but they jump ahead to the solution, often before the person has had a chance to fully understand his or her situation and feel their feelings. Healing is a *process* and it should not be short-circuited. This ill-timed approach actually depends on a shallow view of the problem of evil: If God is good and all-powerful, why is there evil? Or, to state it another way: If God is love and he can do anything, why can't he keep me from feeling this pain? The problem solver's approach is to deny the evil, or at least minimize it: Your pain isn't very important, because it's only temporary—there's a greater good ahead of you. Thus there's no problem of evil because there's no real evil.

That's cheating. What if, for instance, you had tickets to the World Series and someone said, "You don't need to go to the game. I'll just tell you who wins"? That wouldn't be quite the same, even though the end result would be the same (that is, knowing who wins). You are richer for the experience of watching the game, not just knowing its outcome. Have you ever seen a movie or play with someone who had already seen it? At a suspenseful moment, you don't want your companion to lean over and say, "The butler did it." You want the entire richness of the viewing experience—including all the questions and uncertainty involved in the process.

So we're not saying that Bible verses such as Romans 8:28 are bad or wrong. Actually, you can find a helpful line of hope and reasoning in this and other Bible passages. But we must not deal with human suffering by denying it or by short-circuiting the healing process. Such an approach is like putting a Band-Aid on a gaping wound. Many people use the Bible sensitively and insightfully in dealing with these tough questions; we just don't recommend the quick-fix approach to pain and suffering.

The Question of Suffering

Let's look deeper into this question of suffering. Many have tried to answer it, and we might learn from some of their attempts.

The problem, again, has three elements: God's love, God's power, and human suffering. Any two of those go together fairly easily, but it's hard to believe in the coexistence of all three simultaneously. As we've seen, the problem solvers deny or minimize the suffering. Others seem to give either God's love or his power short shrift.

Some theologians have recently presented a God who is unable to stop evil. He's very loving, and he tries to help us in our difficulty, but he really can't be blamed, because he's not in charge. Still others focus on God's power but neglect God's love. This is a danger in the fire-and-brimstone emphasis of some Christians: God punishes evil. We get what we deserve. Within this system, people live in fear of an awesome God, but they don't sense his love for them.

It is difficult to maintain the balance among all three elements. But there have been attempts to explain human suffering with a balanced approach. We'll try to encapsulate some of these theories here.

Individual Sin

The first general explanation is that we bring on our own suffering by sinning. This theory has two angles: individual and corporate. The individual view is rather straightforward: sin has consequences, and you eventually suffer for your misdeeds. It's not necessarily that God zaps you for being bad, though some would suggest this. It's usually that the sin itself brings suffering. For example, a guy gets drunk and drives into a tree. His injuries result directly from his drunken driving. From his hospital bed, he may cry out, "Why, oh why, Lord, are you letting me suffer like this?" But he's forgetting his own destructive behavior.

Not all cases are so clear-cut. A man might give his all to his job in order to become professionally successful. There are late nights, weekends spent writing reports, phone calls, and business trips that take him away from his family. Work has become his god. When his wife tells him that she wants a divorce, he cries out to God in despair. But hasn't this man created this situation himself, at least in part?

Sometimes people get mad at God for not saving them from their own folly. When they face the painful consequences of their own choices, they blame God. Is that reasonable? What kind of God do they want?

Consider the parent who gives a child choices, but then always smooths out the consequences. Let's say that Bobby gets a five-dollar allowance for the week and blows it all on candy the first day. The next day, Bobby is crying because the money is gone and he wants more candy. Should the parent shrug and say, "Okay, here's more money"? You may know some parents like that, but it's hardly the loving approach. It's best for the child when the parent says, "No, you'll get more money next week, and then maybe you won't spend it all at once." The child needs to learn—and so do we—that choices have consequences.

We may never know how often God *does* protect us from bad consequences; we just know when he doesn't. According to this theory of suffering, we should learn from our self-induced pain rather than blaming God for it.

That sounds good, but it doesn't cover all cases. In fact, it explains only a small portion of human suffering. It covers the drunk driver, but not the little girl that the drunk driver hits. What was her sin? Crossing the street?

Corporate Sin

The corporate-sin theory holds that we all share in the consequences of human sin. Since Eden, we are a fallen race. One sin has led to another until the whole fabric of human interaction has been intricately woven with the consequences of sin. The little girl mentioned earlier bears the weight of the drunk driver's sins. The Armenians suffer for the Turks' sins.

At first, that doesn't seem to help a whole lot. It's still unfair! How can a loving God let that happen?

It comes back to choices and consequences. If God gives people real choices to make, he has to let them make their choices. If he allows people to choose his way of peace or their own way of violence, and they choose violence, he can't call off the game. He has set up a system in which people choose, every day, to do right or wrong. Some will do wrong, and that sometimes means that they'll victimize innocent people. God doesn't want them to make such choices, but what's the alternative? Make them robots? Program their behavior?

Imagine a computer that is programmed to greet you each morning by saying, "You're great! You're wonderful! I love you!" How affirmed would that make you feel? Not much, we'd guess, because the computer has no choice but to say those words. The words therefore have no meaning. That same principle holds for our relationship with God. If we could only choose good, that wouldn't really be a choice. The whole concept of "good" would be meaningless. It would just be something we were programmed to do.

According to the corporate-sin view, God has given all of us a beautiful gift of choice. Some choose wrongly, and we all must suffer for that. We can only hope that God will make it up to the innocent victims in the future—whether in this life or the next.

But some might press the point that there are no innocent victims. We are all sinners, in one way or another. The little girl may not have caused the drunk-driving accident that injured her, but she has certainly made other selfish choices that have contributed to the fabric of human sin.

This makes some sense, but it sounds pretty harsh. Many people would still see a lack of love in a God who lets a little girl get hurt because of the "fabric of human sin." So let's look at another explanation.

Silver Lining

Sometimes our suffering has a silver lining. For instance, Michele's son Jarryd didn't make his junior high school basketball team, though he had been playing basketball since he was five and nurtured hopes of being an NBA star. This saddened him greatly, and it angered him, because he felt he played better than some of the coach's favorites. Still, he got cut from the squad and raged about the injustice . . . until some friends invited him to join the wrestling team.

This turned out to be a much better fit. Jarryd liked the kids on this other team more, and he showed considerable talent. Though Jarryd had never wrestled before, the coach said he was among the best he'd seen. He finished the season with a pile of trophies!

You can see the silver lining here. The pain of getting cut from the basketball team was substantial, but if that hadn't happened, he would never have discovered his talent for wrestling. The same thing can happen in our lives. As the old saying goes, when God closes one door, he opens another. We don't like getting doors slammed in our faces, but often the result is better for us.

One thinks of Joni Eareckson Tada, paralyzed as a teenager in a diving accident. It was a tragedy, no question about it, and she spent a good deal of time questioning God's goodness. But she came out of her tragic experience with a closer relationship to God and a ministry to others, especially other hurting people. She has found success as an artist, a musician, an author, and a speaker that she would never have found without that fateful accident.

We don't mean to deny or minimize the pain and suffering involved in bad experiences, but often the worst things turn out to be the best things. That's hard to believe when you're in the middle of the difficulty, but it has happened again and again in people's lives. God has good things in store for you, but you often need to pass through some pain.

This is essentially the message of the problem solvers, though their insensitivity and timing may make it hard to accept. All things *do* work together for good for those who love God. God *does* have a purpose, but you may have to go through some hard times to get there.

Testing

But why? Why does everything have to be so painful? Why can't God just give us the good things without the suffering? Doesn't he have that power?

It's not about power, but about purpose, some would reply. God is molding us, building us up, growing us. Our suffering is a kind of test, a crucible in which we're heated up and purified. We become stronger through crisis—isn't that true? Look around at the people you respect the most. Aren't they the ones who have gone through hard times and emerged with greater wisdom, greater vision, greater character?

In college, I (Randy) edited the school literary magazine. I asked my brilliant but cynical friend Jeff to serve as poetry editor. Once, as we evaluated a poem submitted by a classmate, Jeff said, "It's very sweet, but she's never suffered. She needs some pain in her life." It was true. The poet was a lovely, talented young woman whose life had been pretty easy up to then. And her poem was nicely worded—like a greeting card. It had no edge to it, no power, no character. Of course the editor wasn't really wishing pain on anyone, but he recognized that the best poetry came from people whose lives were more difficult.

The New Testament speaks frequently about the value of testing. "Consider it pure joy, my brothers, whenever you face trials of many kinds," says James, "because you know that the testing of your faith develops perseverance. Perseverance must finish its work so that you may be mature and complete, not lacking anything" (James 1:2-4). Paul seconds the motion: "We also rejoice in our sufferings, because we know that suffering produces perseverance; perseverance, character; and character, hope" (Romans 5:3-4).

Rejoicing in suffering? That might seem a bit much but we're not talking about denial here. Suffering hurts—it's supposed to. How else will it produce perseverance? This "joy" the Bible talks about is not merely tranquility or even common happiness. It's a broader vision, one that sees the mountains ahead while you're trudging through the valley.

So in this view, God has the power to keep you from suffering, but he lovingly allows you to suffer so that you can grow.

The Hereafter

We want to mention one more variation on these themes. Some people remind us that this world is not our home—or, in the words of the old spiritual, "We're just a-passin' through." Our earthly existence may be full of suffering, but a better life awaits us.

That may strike you as escapist, but it's really quite a reasonable way to look at life. We humans wonder how a loving and powerful God could let us go through suffering—but what if this present suffering is just a blip in the bliss of eternity? That can change our perspective entirely.

When Jesus warned his disciples about the persecution they would face, he counseled, "Do not be afraid of those who kill the body but cannot kill the soul. Rather, be afraid of the One who can destroy both soul and body in hell" (Matthew 10:28). The point is that there are worse things than physical suffering. There are more important planes of life. We can mourn the untimely death of an innocent person in an accident, and we can rail against the injustice of it. But if God is merely moving a person from this life to the next, can we really call that unjust? If God is bringing that person into his own glorious presence, is that such a tragedy—at least when viewed from the perspective of eternity?

In the (sanitized) words of a popular bumper sticker, "Stuff happens, and then you die." But according to the biblical view of the hereafter, the last part of that sentence is a promise, not a threat. For the believer, death brings a whole new existence in close proximity to God. As Paul wrote, "I consider that our present sufferings are not worth comparing with the glory that will be revealed in us" (Romans 8:18). Helen's father was killed for his refusal to deny God. This ended his life on earth. But what glory awaited him?

This view may still seem escapist to you. Maybe you feel it doesn't answer your questions. This "loving" God still allows earthly pain, or is powerless to stop it. Why?

Jesus offered an interesting word picture that might help us:

> *"The kingdom of heaven is like a man who sowed good seed in his field. But while everyone was sleeping, his enemy came and sowed weeds among the wheat, and went away. When the wheat sprouted and formed heads, then the weeds also appeared. The owner's servants . . . asked him, 'Do you want us to go and pull [the weeds] up?'*
>
> *"'No,' he answered, 'because while you are pulling the weeds, you may root up the wheat with them. Let*

both grow together until the harvest. At that time I
will tell the harvesters: First collect the weeds and tie
them in bundles to be burned; then gather the wheat
and bring it into my barn.'" (Matthew 13:24-30)

According to this parable, we are currently in that middle period when wheat and weeds are growing together. Good and bad coexist in our world, and often the bad victimizes the good. God is not ignoring this situation, but is allowing it to happen *for now*. At "the harvest," he will make things right.

We don't know whether any of these explanations will calm your anger. Maybe a combination of two or three of them will ring true with you. Maybe as you reexamine the issues these rationales will change your perspective; maybe not.

Remember that anger is a natural response to a *perceived* injustice. But perceptions can be wrong. Sometimes we get angry over a misunderstanding. Once we get the whole story and realize that our anger was unfounded, it becomes easy to let go of it.

Say you're walking across the street and suddenly some guy tackles you. You're knocked to the ground, bones bruised, clothing torn, knees and elbows skinned. You pick yourself up, gearing for a fight. What was this guy doing? He had no reason to knock you down! How dare he attack you in this way!

But then you turn and see a tractor-trailer racing past you, right where you would have been if this strange guy had not tackled you. You had not seen it coming. You were daydreaming as you set out across the street, but this man pushed you out of harm's way. Now you realize he saved your life. So instead of punching him, you're hugging him. What changed? Only how you saw the situation.

What if you had never turned to see the truck race past? What if you had never realized that this man had saved your life? You might think you were totally justified in attacking the man who helped you. You might lash out in anger against the very person who protected you from harm.

We're asking you to consider that this might be the situation you're in with God. Granted, you feel wounded and it seems to you that God must be the culprit. But maybe he is saving you from some greater harm. Maybe the whole human race is preoccupied with crossing the street against the light, and we deserve to be smashed flat by the consequences of our sin. Maybe God is our rescuer.

Job and Friends

The book of Job asks many of the same questions we're asking. Thought to be one of the oldest pieces of Hebrew literature we have, it is tucked away in the middle of the Old Testament, the first of the five "books of wisdom" (along with Psalms, Proverbs, Ecclesiastes, and Song of Songs). All of these books ask basic questions about human existence. Job focuses on suffering.

As this story goes, God allows the Tempter to torment a righteous man named Job. He loses his substantial wealth, his family, and his health. "Curse God and die!" his wife barks on her way out the door, but Job refuses to speak out against his Creator. As he sits in the trash pile scraping the boils on his skin, three friends come to console him.

As luck would have it, these friends are philosophers. For about thirty chapters, they present their explanations for Job's woes. Generally, they accuse him of bringing his suffering upon himself through some sin he's hiding or unaware of. Job tries to defend himself; he will not take the rap.

Then a fourth philosopher appears, a young whippersnapper named Elihu, who challenges them all to focus on God's greatness: "The Almighty is beyond our reach and exalted in power; in his justice and great righteousness, he does not oppress" (37:23).

And finally God speaks up, basically agreeing with Elihu. "Where were you when I laid the earth's foundation?" he asks (38:4). For a few more chapters, he lists his accomplishments— all the great things he has created. The idea is: "How can you sec-ond-guess me when you don't even know how to make a giraffe?"

In response, Job admits, "Surely I spoke of things I did not understand, things too wonderful for me to know" (42:3).

At face value, this doesn't seem very helpful. The lesson of the book seems to be the sort of thing the problem solvers might give you: *Don't ask questions; just accept.* After all this back-and-forth about suffering, God finally shows up—*and he doesn't answer the question!* Job and his friends are asking, "Why, God, why?" and God responds, basically, "You wouldn't understand."

Philip Yancey, who has written much on the subject of suffer-ing, points out that the book of Job is not about *suffering*, but about *faith.* The book starts with a wager between God and the Devil: *Will Job lose his faith?* Despite all his suffering, Job kept his faith and won the bet for God. He never figured things out, but he still trusted God.[2]

And that explains God's "answer." He never explains the reason for Job's sufferings, but he asserts his own majesty. Job is in no position to judge the justice of God's actions. God is God and Job is not—nor are we.

Based on this, we might conclude that it's not important to find an explanation for suffering. There will always be things we don't understand, things "too wonderful for us to know," but God is still there for us, powerful enough to create a world and loving enough to want a relationship with us.

C. S. Lewis dealt with this issue in his classic *Mere Christianity,* admitting that he had been an atheist for quite a while because of his struggle with the question of evil:

> My argument against God was that the universe seemed so cruel and unjust. But how had I got this

idea of *just* and *unjust?* A man does not call a line
crooked unless he has some idea of a straight line.[3]

The answer to Lewis's question about the origin of justice is,
of course, God. He has given us the sense of what's right and just
and fair. He is the author of justice. So how can we accuse him
of injustice? The very sense of justice that fuels our anger against
him is a gift from him! Our best choice is to conclude that we just
don't have enough information. God must be doing something
that we don't understand yet.

We can still be frustrated with the *seeming* injustice. We certainly wish we had all the answers. And we can share these feelings freely with God, as Job and other people of faith have. But
we shouldn't let our justice-seeking anger drive us away from the
Author of justice.

CHAPTER THREE

WHY ME?

First the men, then the boys. The Turkish authorities were methodical in their annihilation of the Armenian people. Helen had seen her father die at gunpoint and heard the screams when her brother died, locked with other Armenian youths in a burning building. Now only women and children were left.

Helen and her mother and younger sisters were herded with thousands of other Armenian women on a march across the desert. Some sense of chivalry (or public relations) kept the Turkish soldiers from massacring them. They let the natural elements perform the executions.

In a book called *Silences,* a woman named Frances tells a story that remarkably parallels Helen's. Frances, too, traveled with her mother and sister on that death march. "Forced on the march, we walked and walked and walked. We did not know where we were going. . . . 'God will take care of us,' [my mother] consoled as if in prayer. I was silent. I could not reach her God."[1]

In the same way, twelve-year-old Helen questioned the faith that her mother clung to. Through the desert march, Helen's mother kept praying and praising. Helen would have none of that.

Frances describes the forced march through difficult terrain:

> When we were in the hills, climbing treacherous roads,
> the rod of the enemy was at our back. I was scared.
> One false step and I would be in the bottomless abyss

below. Many fell and we heard their cries, but none of us could help them. We had to continue or be stuck with the end of their gun. . . .

For many days, it must have been many months, we kept walking. Many died of hunger and thirst. Then we came to a desert. We walked under the hot, August sun; I was tired. We were hot by day and so very cold at night.[2]

Helen's four-year-old sister, Berjouhi, died on the march. Prevented by soldiers from burying her child, Helen's mother quickly threw some sand over the girl's body and kept walking. Helen looked back to see a pack of wild dogs eating the corpse. She vomited and then spat in anger—at both the God she blamed and her mother, who kept praying to him. Her six-year-old sister, Elksop, died next from lack of food and water. Helen had seen the deaths of four members of her family. Only she and her mother were left.

In her book *Silences,* Frances tells how her sister wandered off to look for water. When she didn't return, her mother went to look for her. Neither of them ever returned, and Frances was left alone. "It is very hard to be alone," Frances says. "One cannot imagine what it was like at such a young age to have no one. What kind of God is it who allows the innocent to suffer? What kind of God left me alone with no one who cared whether I lived or died?"[3]

Those are the questions that seared Helen's soul, too, as she marched hundreds of miles through the Armenian desert with her mother, stepping over the dead bodies that littered their path. But then Helen's story took a turn. A Turkish officer who had been herding this group took a liking to Helen. When he left his assignment, he decided to take her with him.

Helen was never sure which was the frying pan and which was the fire. She was spared the torturous, possibly deadly, march through the desert, but she was separated from her mother and forced to live with this enemy officer. And she was still but a child.

Facing the Facts

Face it. God just doesn't perform up to our expectations. When you trust in God, you expect him to save you from disasters like the Armenian Genocide, like the Holocaust, like the Columbine High School shooting, or like the Oklahoma City bombing. People of faith make all kinds of excuses for him, but the truth is, he doesn't always come through for us.

Whatever shred of faith Helen retained from her family heritage was left there in the desert. Her mother trudged onward, still trusting in this strangely absent God. Helen was whisked out of her childhood and forced to live as a wife to her worst enemy. If this was how God treated his own people, maybe it was better to be one of his *enemies*.

And maybe those thoughts have crossed your mind, too. Oh, maybe you've kept up appearances, going to church, praying the prayers—but somewhere along the line you learned that those prayers don't always get answered. The faithful ones keep crowing about the goodness of God, but you haven't seen it on any consistent basis. Yes, there are occasional "miracles," but what good are they when they're sprinkled among so many disasters? A church might celebrate when someone's cancer goes into remission, calling it a great act of God—but shouldn't they blame God when the cancer returns a year later, pulling the patient into a slow, painful death?

You can blindly, blithely ignore the problems, pretending that God always provides healing and happiness—or you can face the facts. If you have been disillusioned by a God who didn't turn out as you expected, you're not the only one. Many who grew up singing "God Is So Good" have been hurt by bad events that God allowed. Some have chosen to ignore the contradictions and cling to a childlike faith. Some have scrapped their faith entirely. Some have wandered somewhere between those two extremes, wondering how to put that all together.

Disappointment

Psychologically, there are several steps in the disillusionment process, whether one is disillusioned with the behavior of a friend, an institution, or God.

First is the basic disappointment. High hopes are smashed flat. Positive feelings are exchanged for negative ones—or at least feelings of uncertainty. Can you count on this friend to be there for you? Can you continue to belong to this club, this group of friends, this church? Is God still worthy of your trust? Things you once took for granted are now shaky.

Disappointment is largely a revision of your vision. You see matters differently. Your friends, your faith, your future—all are cast in a new light when disappointment hits. When it's God you're disappointed in, all the old Sunday school images start to fade. You just don't know who he is anymore.

There's also a heaviness that comes with disappointment. Hopes are buoyant, lifting you up, bringing you joy in your relationships. But disappointment brings you down—literally, sometimes. Your shoulders stoop, your head hangs. Whatever energy you were going to invest in the relationship with the one who has disappointed you—well, that energy dissipates like air released from a balloon. When God is the object of your disappointment, you find yourself drained of joy. The congregation might sing its bubbly choruses all around you, but you're just mouthing the words, if that. You might go through the motions, but it's just too hard to get excited anymore.

In his book *Disappointment with God*, Philip Yancey describes some of the times when he felt God was letting him down. You may be familiar with these feelings:

> Petty disappointments tend to accumulate over time, undermining my faith with a lava flow of doubt. I start to wonder whether God cares about everyday

details—about me. I am tempted to pray less often, having concluded in advance that it won't matter. Or will it? My emotions and my faith waver.[4]

Vicki, a bubbly nine-year-old, was walking home from school as she usually did each day, when a strange car pulled alongside her. Quickly she was pulled into the car, raped, and then thrown onto the street. Now as a middle-aged woman, she still wonders how God could let that happen: "I've been going to church all these years, going through the motions. Just going through the motions. You know, I'm angry at him for allowing this to happen!"

Saying this was actually a major breakthrough for Vicki. Many people of faith have such feelings, but don't want to admit them. They feel the heaviness, their lives drained of joy, but they refuse to say that God has disappointed them. Honest admissions like Yancey's self-description seem scandalous to such people. How can a perfect God disappoint anyone?

People's emotional progress is stunted by their fear of being theologically incorrect. There is a way through these feelings, but you have to keep moving. When you're crying out in distress, you don't stop to run the spell-check program. Our psychological pre-scription throughout this book is pretty simple, really: *Feel your feelings first and then work through the theology later.*

And that's basically what we find in the Bible. The prophet Jeremiah wasn't shy about communicating his disappointment with God:

> *O Hope of Israel,*
> *its Savior in times of distress,*
> *why are you like a stranger in the land,*
> *like a traveler who stays only a night?*
> *Why are you like a man taken by surprise,*
> *like a warrior powerless to save?*

> *You are among us, O LORD,*
> *and we bear your name;*
> *do not forsake us!* (Jeremiah 14:8-9)

The prophet didn't stop there. He went on to grapple with the issues, but he wasn't afraid to feel his feelings first. The same could be said of the psalmists. In Psalm 73, for instance, the writer freely complains about the prosperity of the wicked (and his own poverty). Later he goes to the "sanctuary of God" and gains new insight there. We can benefit from his insights, to be sure, but first we need to own up to our feelings of disappointment.

Betrayal

The next emotional step is usually a sense of betrayal—and here's where anger rears its head. While disappointment is a vague dissipation of hope, this sense of betrayal is specifically targeted. *You hurt me! You didn't keep your promises! You double-crossed me! You are responsible for my pain!* Betrayal brings blame.

Anger is based on a sense of justice, so this adds fuel to the negative feelings. You are disappointed when others don't meet your expectations. You feel betrayed when people fail to meet their responsibilities. Betrayal implies a contract of some kind, written or assumed, with certain obligations.

In a marriage, you feel disappointed when your spouse doesn't help with the dishes; you feel betrayed when your spouse has an affair. The marriage contract—"forsaking all others"—has been broken.

A close friendship carries certain assumptions of loyalty. When these are broken—when you find a friend gossiping about you or rejecting you in favor of others—you feel wronged. You let this person into your heart, entrusting him with your love, but he has used that trust to cause you pain. That's not right.

The most famous betrayer of them all, Judas Iscariot, used his position as a friend to turn Jesus over to those who crucified him. He scrapped his commitment to be Jesus' friend in order to get money.

In business, most deals are put in writing. Betrayal of such agreements is "breach of contract" and actionable in a lawsuit. But there are also many handshakes, hints, and hallway promises. The middle manager rightly feels betrayed when passed over for a promotion she was in line for. There's no written contract, just an understanding—but that was violated, and the victim is seething.

What happens when it seems that God has betrayed you?

If you were touchy about the idea of God *disappointing* you, you'll hate this notion. Surely, God is good and faithful and true. How could he ever betray someone? How could God break a promise? But remember that we're talking about *feelings*. We *feel* that God has betrayed us, and we're angry about what we *see* as a contractual breach. We have trusted God to protect us, to answer our prayers, and to give us joy. When it seems that those duties are left undone, we feel betrayed.

We'll talk later about the nature of that "contract" with God, but let's stay on this emotional track for now. How does it feel to be betrayed? We feel anger, of course, but also shock. How could this trusted friend cause us such pain? The love we have felt in the past makes the betrayal even more painful. Not only are we mistreated, but we're mistreated by the very one we expected to treat us well.

Again, the psalmist gives words to our feelings:

> *My God, my God, why have you forsaken me?*
> *Why are you so far from saving me,*
> *so far from the words of my groaning?* (Psalm 22:1)

The forsaking is all the worse because he is "*my* God."

Underneath it all is the sense that *I deserve better.* We're back to contract language: *We had an agreement. I did my part; you didn't.* Jeremiah complained,

> *I never sat in the company of revelers,*
> *never made merry with them;*
> *I sat alone because your hand was on me*
> *and you had filled me with indignation.*
> *Why is my pain unending*
> *and my wound grievous and incurable?*
> *Will you be to me like a deceptive brook,*
> *like a spring that fails?* (Jeremiah 15:17-18)

In other words, this prophet renounced common pleasures because he was busy serving God. Why then was God punishing him rather than rewarding him? It just didn't seem fair.

A number of modern "prophets" might say the same thing. Sure, some people who faithfully serve God lead what appear to be long and blessed lives. But what about the many missionaries who have been killed as they have tried to spread God's love?

Jane had dedicated her life to serving God. An active member of her church, she also ran a women's ministry program for her community. She sacrificed much of her time, energy, talents, and money in the work of the Lord. Why then was her grandchild a victim of sexual abuse? Why didn't God shield her family from harm?

Bad things do happen to good people, to very good people, and that leaves us shaking our heads. Why doesn't God honor his most faithful servants with pain-free lives? Don't they deserve that much? Doesn't he owe a woman like Jane a certain amount of protection for her loved ones?

This sense of entitlement squirts lighter fluid on the fired coals of our feelings. Our disappointment ignites into anger over our apparent betrayal.

Abandonment

Then we just feel alone.

Picture the woman whose husband walks out on her. She's shocked at first, and deeply disappointed. She feels betrayed and angry. How could he do this to her? But the worst thing is that she misses him. It used to be that she could talk with him about her problems. Now he's gone. Now he *is* the problem. When the fire of her rage finally dies down, she feels abandoned, alone.

That's how some people feel about God. When God doesn't live up to our expectations, we feel disappointed with him, betrayed, and angry. So we slam the door on him. If he's not going to treat us right, why should we have anything to do with him?

That's when some decide to become atheists. Others just turn away from anything having to do with God. They stop going to church, reading the Bible, praying. They know God's out there somewhere, but they're punishing him by dropping out of his club. Still others stay in the club and go through the motions of faith, but without any personal interaction with God. They have shut down emotionally, as far as God is concerned.

This sort of thing is common in human relationships. You may know someone who suffered a painful romantic breakup early in life and has refused to fall in love since. After any breakup there's a season when the heart is tender, emotions are fragile, and it's wise to shut down a bit. But some people go years and years without opening their hearts again. They've been hurt; they don't want to be hurt again. Love is a risk, and they prefer to play it safe.

The result is loneliness. Shut people out, and there's no one to play with. Shut God out, and there's no one to pray to. You're on your own. When you've cried out all your anger, you're left alone.

Depression often follows anger. You've spent all your energy railing against your mistreatment—and then what? Your emotional coffers are empty. It's easier not to care about anything, not to love, not to want. You go through life just existing, and even that can be a chore sometimes.

That was the state of mind Helen often found herself in. She was a fighter—no doubt about it—but she'd get mighty tired. Separated from her family, tied to a captor, and holding a grudge against God, she was removed from every possible source of strength. She was convinced that if she were to ever get through this, she would do so on her own. So she plodded down her lonely trail through life.

A Prophet's Rage

Do you see yourself in that emotional portrait? Disappointed? Raging with the anger of betrayal? Or perhaps very lonely? If you're somewhere on that path, you may be wondering where it's leading. Is loneliness the only life you can look forward to?

Not necessarily. Digging deep into the Old Testament, we find the story of Elijah. This thundering prophet stood up for the true God when the whole culture of Israel had joined in the worship of a local fertility god. Elijah had challenged the false prophets to a duel of sorts, seeing who could call down fire from heaven. Hundreds of false prophets tried all day without success, but Elijah prayed and *zap!*—it happened.

An exhilarating victory, right? Not exactly. Queen Jezebel was livid. She threatened to punish Elijah for humiliating her god and her priests. Elijah had to run for his life.

He went south, through the desert, finally camping out in a cave near Mount Sinai. He was depressed, moping, even suicidal:

> And the word of the LORD came to him: "What are you doing here, Elijah?"
> He replied, "I have been very zealous for the LORD God Almighty. The Israelites have rejected your

covenant, broken down your altars, and put your prophets to death with the sword. I am the only one left, and now they are trying to kill me too." (1 Kings 19:9-10)

It's all there: anger at the Lord's apparent injustice, loneliness, a sense of persecution. Elijah had given and given and given, and what did he get in return? Death threats. That wasn't fair! And Elijah found himself in the strange position of challenging the very God he had been fighting for. But there's more:

The LORD said, "Go out and stand on the mountain in the presence of the LORD, for the LORD is about to pass by."
Then a great and powerful wind tore the mountains apart and shattered the rocks before the LORD, but the LORD was not in the wind. After the wind there was an earthquake, but the LORD was not in the earthquake. After the earthquake came a fire, but the LORD was not in the fire. And after the fire came a gentle whisper. (1 Kings 19:11-12)

Here we find a picture of anger-at-God therapy. In psychology we call it *cognitive reframing.* It's basically changing the way you think about things—broadening or deepening your perspective.

As with Job, God doesn't really answer the questions he's asked. Elijah has accused God of mistreating him, of failing to reward him for his faithful service, of abandoning him when the chips were down. In response, God offers the Weather Channel.

A mighty wind, an earthquake, a fire—God was not in any of those spectacular displays. He spoke to Elijah in a "gentle whisper." Remember that Elijah had just called fire from heaven to prove his case before the false prophets. God was certainly capable of flashy actions, but Elijah seemed to be looking for those clear-cut "acts of God" in every aspect of life. *If you can send fire from heaven, why not throw a lightning bolt at the wicked queen?*

That's what we want, too, isn't it? The wind, the earthquake, the fire—we want God to act decisively to mow down the oppressors of the Armenians or the Jews or the Somalians. We want him to shout his mighty truth into the silence, but all we get is this gentle whisper. So instead of being vindicated by big events, we (like Elijah) become people who hear voices that no one else can hear. Instead of gaining the miraculous healing we're praying for, we hear sweet words of comfort in our sleep. That's not exactly the act of God we wanted.

But God doesn't apologize for this. He doesn't explain it. We don't even know what the gentle whisper *said.* All we know is that God presented himself to Elijah in a way totally different from what he expected. Elijah had to change his mind about God.

The biblical stories are helpful because the people in them are so much like us. Elijah doesn't get it at first, just as we so often misunderstand what God is trying to say. After the gentle whisper, God asks Elijah *again,* "What are you doing here?" And the prophet launches into the same tirade—word for word! *I've been zealous, I'm all alone,* and so on. The meteorology lesson has had no effect.

Reframing is never easy, but it's an important step in dealing with our anger against God. We need to evaluate our notions of who we expect him to be and compare them with who he really is.

Often a married couple will seek counseling because they're making each other mad. You'd be surprised how often the problem is simply a matter of expectations. She's mad at him for not taking out the trash. He's mad at her for nagging him to take out the trash. As they explore the issue they realize the conflict stems from their childhood. Her father always took out the trash, so she saw it as the man's work. But in his home, Mom took out the trash, so he assumed it was the woman's work. He would do it, but he resented her complaining—because (as he saw it) it was really her job. She figured he was just lazy, shirking his rightful duties, and she resented his attitude even when he did the job.

It sounds silly, but committed relationships are built on such expectations. She thought she married a trash-hauling husband, and she's disappointed when he turns out different. In other relationships the issue might be cooking, child-rearing, employment, or appearance. As long as people cling to their expectations, those relationships will be in trouble. They need to learn to rewrite the rules, to revise their roles, to create new images based on the reality of the person they married.

The same thing happens with God. When God disappoints us, or when we feel he's betrayed us, it's often because he hasn't been the kind of God we expected. We learn that we can't count on God to meet our expectations, and we nurse our feelings of resentment.

Our Expectations of God

Just as married couples get their ideas of male and female roles from the family of their childhood, so we often develop our understanding of who God is in our childhood. As a result, many of us find a certain childlike quality in our ideas of God.

Santa Claus

One early image that stays with many people into adulthood is jolly old St. Nick himself—Santa Claus. Think about it: a nice old man who gives gifts to children all around the world. But not just any children. He's checking to see "who's naughty and nice." If your behavior doesn't measure up, you'll suffer the indignity of getting coal in your stocking while your brothers and sisters play with their new toys. So there's a sense of justice here, but we learn that just about everybody gets toys from this red-suited demigod—you have to be pretty terrible to get coal.

And that's close to the picture many adults have of God: a jolly old soul who appears now and then to shower us with presents. Good people are rewarded and bad people are supposed to be shamed, but just about everyone makes the grade.

When you see God as Santa Claus, you have good reason to get angry when bad things happen to you, or when you don't get some good thing you really want. It's like getting coal in your stocking after a year of being good. Where's the justice? You're supposed to get toys in exchange for your good behavior. That's what the contract says. God is supposed to check his list twice, and if you've been "good for goodness' sake" he's supposed to bring "lots of toys and goodies on his sleigh." So what happened?

God is not Santa. He never said he would be, certainly not in the Old or New Testament. The Santa Claus myth is a story for children, meant to keep them happy and well-behaved, but not a valid expectation for adults seeking a mature relationship with God.

Are you mad at God for being a bad Santa? If so, you might want to take another look at who God really is.

The Grandfather

C. S. Lewis wrote that what we really want is a God who approves of anything we like doing: "We want, in fact, not so much a Father in Heaven as a grandfather in heaven—a senile benevolence who, as they say, 'liked to see young people enjoying themselves,' and whose plan for the universe was simply that it might truly be said at the end of each day, 'a good time was had by all.'"[5]

Is that closer to your image of God? The difference between parents and grandparents (in most families anyway) is that grandparents have no clout. Parents discipline. Grandparents coddle. Grandma says, "Go ahead and have that cotton candy," when it's Mom who has to deal with the kid's sugar rush, not to mention laundering the shirt. Grandpa is satisfied to chuckle and shake his head when the child disobeys, but Dad can't, because it's his job to teach obedience.

So if you expect a God who spoils you, you'll be upset when he disciplines you. If you want a grandfather, you might be angry when God insists on being your Father.

Grandparents can afford to dote on the grandkids, because they're less involved in their lives. Parents are closer to the kids, more heavily invested in their lives, and so their love takes on a stronger character—and it may not always look like love. A stranger you meet at a party may wish you well, "loving" you by vaguely wanting you to be happy. Only a close friend or relative will love you enough to challenge your behavior. The stranger is more accepting, it might seem, but the friend actually loves you more.

Say Joe is an alcoholic. Monday night he dines at the home of a business associate he hardly knows. Joe asks for a drink, and the associate, being agreeable, gives him one. Tuesday night he dines with his best friend, Frank. Joe asks for a drink and Frank refuses. Which dinner host loves Joe more? The one who treats him more harshly.

So it goes in our human relationships: the closer we get, the more complicated love gets. It's true with God, too. We often want to keep God at arm's length, treating him as a grandfather. We want him to be agreeable and accepting. But is this the kind of love he wants to show us? No, his love is much more complicated than that.

As C. S. Lewis writes, "I should very much like to live in a universe which was governed on such lines [that is, by a 'senile benevolence']. But since it is abundantly clear that I don't, and since I have reason to believe, nevertheless, that God is Love, I conclude that my conception of love needs correction."[6]

Are you angry at God for not being an agreeable enough grandfather? Maybe you need to consider his role as an involved Father and bring some "correction" to your "conception of love."

Traffic Cop

In child development, there comes a time—usually at eight to ten years—when kids are keen on justice. They begin to learn how the world works, how their own society functions, and they strongly support the concept of fair play. They set up systems among their friends where everyone gets a turn. Cheaters get admonished, even ostracized. When people break the rules, they must be punished. Even though these children complain loudly when *they* face punishment, it's important to them that the rules be followed and that justice be enforced.

Many of us carry that sense of justice into adulthood. We may recognize complications in the administration of justice, but we still want the world to function according to rules and standards. That makes it especially maddening to see evil prevail when we slog along doing good without any recognizable reward. Why isn't God punishing the bad guys?

I (Randy) confess that my sense of justice is keenest when I am driving. Speeders, weavers, and tailgaters earn my wrath. When someone buzzes past me doing 90, I nurture the hope that there's a police car just around the bend. Of course it seems there never is. The only time I see a traffic cop is when *I've* lost concentration and let my speed edge upward.

And, as long as I'm confessing, let me add that I'm a hypocrite. I'll rant about someone doing 90 in a 55-mph zone while I'm doing 65. So I'm guilty, too, just not *as* guilty as the objects of my wrath.

Morally speaking, we want God to be a traffic cop, punishing evil and letting us good folks retake the highways. We get upset when it seems that he's spending all his time at the donut shop and letting scofflaws go free.

There are two problems with the "traffic cop" image of God. The first is that God never signed up for that job. Sure, in the Bible God promises that doing evil has its consequences, but seldom does that mean an instant zapping of evildoers. (There are a few biblical instances of such zapping, but these are the exceptions.) What we find in the Bible, in other religious writings, in world history, and in our own experience is that evildoers often pay the wages of their sin much later in life or not at all—at least in this life. As Jesus said in a parable, the weeds grow together with the wheat until the harvest.

So if there has never, ever been a consistent sense of timing in the punishment of the wicked, why should we be angry at God for not playing traffic cop *now?* Nothing in history should cause us to expect that—except that it seems to us like a good way to operate. If we were in charge, bad people would get zapped on the spot and good people would get their just desserts.

But would that really be such a good idea? It's one thing for a parent or teacher to exact instant discipline when the goal is order in the home or classroom. But what if your main desire is to get someone to love you? You can't force love with punishment and rewards. Love has to be a free choice. If God zapped everyone whenever they sinned, they would learn not to sin, but they wouldn't learn to love. Or if God showered blessing on everyone for doing right, people would learn to do right for the wrong reasons. (That's really the story of Job: the Tempter charged that God was essentially buying Job's love, that without all those blessings Job would no longer be true to God. Job's trials actually gave him freedom to love God without thought of reward.) God is much more inclined to the role of passionate wooer than vigilant police officer.

The second problem with the image of God as traffic cop is seen in Randy's confession of hypocrisy on the highway (and don't pretend that you've never had similar thoughts). We want cops to race after the speeders with sirens blaring, but only those who are speeding faster than we are. The truth is that virtually everyone has exceeded the posted speed limit. If we had our wish, and traffic cops were perfectly vigilant, we'd get some tickets ourselves.

And if God zapped sinners, we'd be hurting.

So if you're angry at God for not being a good enough traffic cop, let him off the hook. He doesn't want to wear that uniform. And be very thankful that he doesn't.

Genie

All of us are guilty sometimes of seeing God as a genie, ready to do our bidding if we just rub him the right way. We can go through all sorts of vows and rituals to get what we want, promising God the moon if he'll only grant our requests. (Well, he already has the moon. We usually promise him ourselves in various forms.)

When we view God as our personal genie, we feel a sense of entitlement. As long as we say the magic words—or do the magic rituals, go to church, live righteously, stop drinking, and so on—God owes us an answered prayer.

Counselors William and Kristi Gaultiere have written about the false images of God people have, and they include the "Magic Genie God." Discussing one client, whom they dub "Manipulative Martha," they say, "She felt that she had the hope of getting what she wanted from God only if she did the right things to please him. . . . She felt that if she prayed in a certain way, 'claimed' the right Scripture, or had 'enough' faith, God was obligated to do what she wanted."[7]

Jesus warned about such a view of God: "And when you pray, do not keep on babbling like pagans, for they think they will be heard because of their many words. Do not be like them, for your Father knows what you need before you ask him" (Matthew 6:7-8). Those "pagans" tried to force God's hand with their repetitive prayers, but Jesus brought the issue back to the area of personal relationship. God is not a genie, a robot, or a machine we can turn on and off at will. He's a loving Father who wants to meet our needs, but has a clearer picture of them than we do.

The strange thing is, *sometimes* he answers our requests. Sometimes he gives us exactly what we want. We pray for some specific thing and *bam!*—there it is.

I (Michele) went through a time as a young teenager when I was trying to figure out whether God was really there. I felt like I was swimming upstream in my spiritual journey. No one in my family went to church, and my grandmother, Helen (the one you've been reading about), would spit in anger at the mere mention of God. But one day I boldly asked God, if he was there, to give me a sign so that I could believe. "If you are really there," I prayed, "have me wake up at 7:00 A.M. without an alarm." I thought that was quite a challenge, since I usually slept until 12:00 or 1:00 if someone or something did not wake me.

The next morning I was surprised to find myself awake at exactly 7:00. So I thought that God might have answered my prayer. But then again, perhaps that was just an unusual coincidence. Still not completely convinced, I asked for another sign. I was in junior high and liked a boy that I never had a chance to see. I asked God to have that boy stand by my locker before homeroom. Since he was in a different grade, he was never in my hall; and I would only be in school about five minutes before homeroom. So this was a tall order, but that was my challenge to God.

When I arrived at school the next day, I was shocked to find that boy standing in front of my locker. This was no coincidence! Now I was sure that God was really there. I thanked God for being so patient with me and I apologized for testing him, yet I knew of no other way to believe.

So prayers do get answered in very specific ways, but we get in trouble when we start to expect service like that. In the genie mentality, when God doesn't respond in just the way we want, we feel cheated, as if he welshed on a deal. "I did $x, y,$ and z for you! Why couldn't you do this one thing for me?"

We're like the five-year-old who goes to the corner store for some candy. He grabs a big candy bar from the shelf and plunks a dime on the counter. "Is that enough?" he asks. Well, it's not nearly enough. Big candy bars are going for ninety-five cents these days, but the clerk knows the kid and his family. Kindly, she says, "Sure. Ten cents."

The next day the kid is back. He unloads a fistful of dimes on the counter and says, "I'll take a dozen."

When God is our personal genie, we accept his generosities as givens. We assume he operates on a principle of "Your prayer is my command." As "Manipulative Martha" told the Gaultieres, "I have the right to have God's blessings because I'm his child. When I claim one of God's promises, he's obligated to give it to me. That's just the way it works."[8]

But that view of God is far too small. Do you really want a God who can be manipulated like that?

The apostle Paul, after wrangling through some difficult questions about God's will and human freedom, concluded,

> *Who has ever given to God,*
> *that God should repay him?*
> *For from him and through him and to him are all things.*
> (Romans 11:35-36)

He was paraphrasing the book of Job, in which God says,

> *"Who has a claim against me that I must pay?*
> *Everything under heaven belongs to me."* (41:11)

So if you're angry at God because you rubbed the bottle and he didn't give you three wishes, get a larger picture. He knows what you need better than you do.

All or Nothing

Here's the mental pathway that many people take in their anger at God. Not all people—you may have taken a different route. But please consider whether this outline captures your thought processes.

I expected God to be A.
[A = Santa, Grandpa, Cop, Genie, or any other desirable but unrealistic image.]

Experience has shown me that he's not.
[That is, I haven't received toys, approval, justice, wishes, or whatever.]

That disappoints me, making me feel betrayed, angry, and possibly abandoned.

Since God isn't A, he must be Z.
[Z = an ogre, abuser, harsh disciplinarian, absentee, or even not there.]

And I will respond to him accordingly.
[Taking my anger and ill will to a new level.]

Based on her Christian upbringing, Helen expected God to be a protector, and he wasn't. She watched her father, brother, and sisters die at the hands of nonChristian oppressors, and she felt disappointed, betrayed, and abandoned. It became easier for her to believe that God didn't care or didn't exist. That was her "Z image" of God, and she lived for eighty years with that image.

Your Z image of God may be different. In *Mistaken Identity*, the Gaultieres describe fourteen negative images of God, including the Statue God, the Elitist Aristocrat God, the Pushy Salesman God, the Demanding Drill Sergeant God, and the Unjust Dictator God. "These false gods are often secretly lodged in our subconscious minds and contribute to much of our personal distress," the Gaultieres write. "As secret enemies, they block us from receiving the love of the Real God that could comfort our hurts and encourage us toward personal growth and spiritual maturity."[9]

Whatever Z image you've chosen, it may be based on an all-or-nothing mentality. Finding one extreme unrealistic, you've bounced to the opposite extreme. But neither extreme is true! Neither image realistically portrays the true God. Helen was right to conclude that God was not a protector in the sense that she expected. It would have been wrong for her to deny the experiences she had gone through. But it was equally wrong to conclude that God didn't exist. She could have rejected her A image without going all the way to Z. She could have landed somewhere in the middle at M or N, believing that God allows terrible things to happen for reasons we don't understand, but that he still wants a loving relationship with us.

That's the challenge we present to you. Examine your A image and your Z image. Who did you expect God to be? How did he disappoint you? What new image of God have you adopted? Is there a middle image you could discover as you talk to other believers, as you investigate the Bible, and as you sort honestly through your own experience?

Granted, he hasn't been the kind of God you expected—but did he ever promise to be that kind of God? Maybe you've been expecting too much, or too little, or something completely different from who God really is.

You're like the woman who moved into a new neighborhood—just her and her cat, Alphonse, and her five-year-old Hyundai, which she called Henrietta. Just a few days after the move, she heard the car engine knocking. She didn't know any mechanics in her new town, but fortunately the next morning she saw an ad in the paper that said, "We Fix Cars." She quickly called the number and explained, "My Henrietta is making a strange sound. She's purring just fine when she idles, but then she starts shaking and whining when she goes fast. She definitely needs to be fixed."

To her surprise, this company made house calls, so the woman arranged to leave her garage open for the mechanics while she took a bus to work. It turned out to be one of those days. Her boss yelled at her all day. The bus was slow and crowded, especially on the way home. Her cat was whining and nearly bit her as she opened the garage door.

Eagerly, the woman took her car out for a spin and heard the same sound as before. She stormed into the house, nearly tripping over the disgruntled Alphonse, and furiously dialed the number of the company she had called that morning.

"My car is no better than before. You've got a lot of nerve putting out an ad that says 'We Fix Cars.'"

A confused clerk stammered on the other end of the phone, "Th-that must have been a typo. We fix *cats*."

The woman was justifiably upset about the condition of her car, but she was very wrong in her expectations. If she had taken care to listen to what kind of service the company was offering, she would have had a better perspective.

It's a silly story, to be sure, but we're the same way with God sometimes. We get a mistaken notion of who God is supposed to be, and then we're mad at him for not being that. If we'd let him tell us the kind of God he wants to be, we'd have a better attitude.

"Imagine a set of people all living in the same building," writes C. S. Lewis. "Half of them think it is a hotel, the other half think it is a prison. Those who think it is a hotel might regard it as quite intolerable, and those who thought it was a prison might decide it was surprisingly comfortable."[10] Your expectations determine much of your response to reality.

Maybe we do our children a disservice by teaching them about a Santa Claus God. Our efforts to portray a pleasant God who makes everything nice may ultimately backfire. As we grow up, we must realize God is more than niceness. Even his awesome love for us has mysterious and frightening aspects. He loves us, but that's not always a picnic in the park. "If you think of this world as a place intended simply for our happiness," Lewis continues, "you find it quite intolerable: think of it as a place of training and correction and it's not so bad."[11]

In his book *Making Sense Out of Suffering,* philosopher Peter Kreeft further promotes this mature view of life:

> The point of our lives in this world is not comfort, security, or even happiness, but training; not fulfillment but preparation. It's a lousy home, but it's a fine gymnasium. . . . The universe is a soul-making machine, a womb, an egg. Jesus didn't make it into a rose garden when he came, though he could have. Rather, he wore the thorns from this world's gardens.[12]

He never promised us a rose garden. He has promised us *himself.* What does that mean? Who *is* he? These are the questions we struggle with. We can throw our energy into wrestling with God, like Jacob of old. "Please tell me your name," Jacob begged, but his divine opponent would not (Genesis 32:29). God might still be maddeningly mysterious to us, but he's there, wrestling with us.

Many marriages reach a point of disillusionment when "the honeymoon is over," and sometimes this explodes into displays of anger. About a year after the wedding, it's common to hear either or both partners saying, "Who *is* this person I married?" As they dated, became engaged, and through the honeymoon and the first year or so, both of them were putting their best foot forward. But that gets tiring, and eventually people decide to let it all hang out—sometimes literally. And that neatly groomed young man starts walking around in a tattered T-shirt, scratching himself. That beautiful bride takes forever to get out of the bathroom in the morning. All the sweet "honeybunches" and "sweethearts" of the early days are replaced by "Hey, do you mind? I'm trying to watch TV!" Welcome to reality.

Some relationships don't make it through the disillusionment process. The people split up, convinced that aliens took over the body of their spouse on the flight back from the honeymoon. But others take the challenge to find out who their spouse really is, to engage in a strenuous process of discovery, exploration, negotiation, and communication. It's not easy, and they're often tempted to bail, but they stay with it. There are fights sometimes, when they scream out their disappointment, but each fight brings a new discovery, and they stay together, the two slowly becoming one.

What is your relationship with God like? Did the naïve expectations of your honeymoon period crash and burn when you faced real conflict? Do you find yourself wondering, *Who is this God I'm supposed to be worshiping?* Does he seem like a stranger to you now?

You can bail if you want. Call the whole thing off. Say the God thing was a big mistake. Or you can take the challenge to find out who he really is, to engage in a strenuous process of discovery, exploration, negotiation, and communication. It's not easy, and you'll still get angry sometimes, but each wrestling session will bring a new discovery.

Disillusionment is to be expected. Childhood images will get shattered. But what will you do with reality?

A CHANCE FOR FREEDOM

"Come quickly. We can escape now if we hurry. Don't take any-thing with you or they will come after you. Hurry!"

Helen's cousin was at the door at midnight, whispering fran-tically. Freedom was available, if she acted now. She could once again be with her own people, the Armenians, not a slave girl among the Turks.

For several years now, Helen had been living in Constantinople (now Istanbul) as a "wife" of the Turkish officer who grabbed her out of the desert. He was not a harsh master, but neither was he a husband she loved. Although he was generally kind to her, this was still slavery. She was glad to be out of the desert, glad to have food and shelter, but she wanted her freedom. She wanted to be around other Armenians. She was very lonely.

By chance, she had run across a cousin in town. She asked about old friends and relatives. The news was scarce; when there was information, it was mostly bad news. Some fortunate ones had used bribery or other influence to emerge unscathed. Some had fled to the cities to gain anonymity. But mostly the news was devastating. Armenian men had been executed on false charges. The murderous spectacle that killed Helen's father had been enacted in many other Armenian villages as well. The young men of the Armenian army had been rounded up and killed, too. Women and children had wandered through the desert, many falling along the way, some taken in as slaves.

Only a few made it safely across the desert. There were sketchy reports of some who had managed to emigrate, legally or not, to other lands — Bulgaria, Syria, even America.

Helen wasn't free to talk much, but her cousin was a welcome link to her old life. Still, the encounter was bittersweet. She had steeled herself against the pain of her situation, shutting down her grief and anger. Helen had no hopes for the future, just a grim determination to get through each day. Now her cousin had reawakened memories of the past and hope for the future. She wasn't sure she wanted to feel those feelings again.

But now, suddenly, there was a knock at the door and an opportunity for escape. Helen could leave this Turkish home and live safely among fellow Armenians, but she had to act *now*. No time to weigh the pros and cons. No time to pack up her possessions. The window of opportunity was closing. "Come quickly," her cousin was saying. "We can escape now if we hurry."

She chose to follow her cousin to freedom. For the second time in her young life, Helen was rousted out of her home on short notice, forced to leave everything behind — including the young son she had given birth to.

Helen never talked much about her child. She denied his existence. Even the children she bore later never knew of Helen's first son until after her death. But she thought about him a lot. He was her child, but also a Turkish child. If she spirited him away, the officer would make every effort to reclaim his heir, and Helen wouldn't have a chance. Turkish law didn't care much for maternal rights or Armenian rights. If she was caught, she certainly would be considered a kidnapper and put to death.

Besides, what kind of life would her son have? She was fleeing to an uncertain freedom. Would she have food, shelter, clothing? Helen was willing to run the risk for herself, but how could she ask this of a baby? She knew the baby would be taken care of in Constantinople. He'd have all the comforts the officer could provide. And with her out of the way, everyone might forget that this baby was half Armenian. He'd have a much better chance in life as a Turk.

She kept telling herself these things as she fled into the cold, dark night.

Her Story and Yours

We're telling Helen's story as a stark example of the process many people go through. In the last chapter, we showed how disappointment and anger with God can lead to feelings of betrayal and abandonment. People then learn to live in that emotional solitude, rejecting God because they feel God has rejected them. This was where Helen found herself as she lived in Constantinople. The immediate danger was dispelled, but she was doomed to live as a stranger in a strange land. Her loneliness was compounded by turning away from God. Many people find that prayer sustains them in difficult times, but she rejected that option.

When people shut God out of their lives, there are several possible emotional results. For some, it can lead to a general feeling of *deep sadness,* of life's intolerable weight. People mask this sadness in a variety of ways. Some indulge in drugs or drink or nonstop partying. Play the music loud enough and you can't hear yourself weeping. Some try very hard to be busy all the time, as if they're afraid to be alone. When God is out of the picture, being alone is being *very* alone.

For others, their sense of abandonment leads to *cynicism.* They become quick to point out every flaw in the world around them. When anyone around them is cheerful, hopeful, or enthusiastic, these cynics try to dampen their spirits. Their verbal needles puncture many balloons. Unfortunately, their high-and-mighty attitude sometimes gains a grudging respect from the people they attack, as if the cynics really do know it all. But such a critical attitude often masks a deep sense of despair. Since God is not in his heaven, nothing is right with the world.

Still others just grow *weary*. Determined to live life without the God who abandoned them when they needed him most, they work very hard to fend for themselves. That can wear a person out.

There are many sad, cynical, weary people who have condemned themselves to languish in a prison of their own making. There's a knocking at the door, a promise of escape and ultimate freedom, but they won't answer. They're afraid. They've been hurt before. They promise themselves they won't hope anymore.

Hidden Rage

Some people don't realize how angry they are. In many corners of our civilized culture, people learn not to show their anger and certainly not to admit being angry, especially when God is the object of their anger.

"The taboos against our feeling and expressing anger are so powerful that even *knowing* when we are angry is not a simple matter," writes Harriet Lerner. "Because the very possibility that we are angry often meets with rejection and disapproval from others, it is no wonder that it is hard for us to know, let alone admit, that we are angry."[1]

William Gaultiere encountered an interesting dilemma in conducting therapy with a number of Christian clients. He discovered that they are angry at God, yet feel as if anger is a sin and anger at God is an even bigger sin—in fact, some consider it blasphemy.

> Consequently, they banish their anger into their subconscious and try to hide their terrible secret from themselves, others, and even God. Once their anger at God is hidden, it festers into a sore of resentment and bitterness which infects their emotional and spiritual lives; their emotions get clogged up inside and their

relationship with God becomes sterile and void of intimacy. Often, to just mention to such people that they may be angry at God causes them to rush to God's defense and piously proclaim His innocence.[2]

Does this denial make the anger go away? No! I (Michele) often use with my clients the image of a huge elephant sitting in the room, with no one wanting to notice the elephant. Although ridiculous, that is often what people who are angry with one another do—they deny feelings of anger. That is also what people who are angry with God often do. Many people are afraid to address any negative feelings with God. So the elephant [anger] is in the room, effectively blocking their relationship with God. No matter how much you deny it, the elephant is still there. You may call it a vase or an end table, but it's still a big elephant in the middle of the room.

And people who are angry at God still go through the emotional processes we've described, *even if they don't realize that anger is fueling all of it.* They feel betrayed and abandoned. They feel as if no one cares about them. They become sad, cynical, and weary. The whole time, they keep paying lip service to God. They assert that God is good and loving; they just feel a bit distant from him. In fact, this unadmitted anger often causes a serious dissonance in their thinking, which goes something like this:

- ≪ God is good and loving;
- ≪ But something terrible has happened to me that I don't deserve;
- ≪ Therefore God is not good and loving;
- ≪ But he must be;
- ≪ So I must have deserved this terrible event;
- ≪ But I know I didn't;
- ≪ So I'm angry about this injustice;
- ≪ But I can't be angry at God;

- (Because he must be good and loving);
- So I must be wicked to feel this way;
- But I'm not wicked;
- So I must not feel angry at God;
- (But I really am angry;
- So maybe I am wicked;
- Which might explain why the terrible thing happened to begin with).

You can see the self-doubt, the God-doubt, and the emotional conflict in this train of thought. So goes the turmoil in the soul of the one who is angry at God but can't admit it. The anger quickly turns into guilt, which is even more effective at removing a person from an intimate relationship with God. People fear that anger will make them God's enemy, but actually guilt is more devastating because it makes God a stranger. As B. B. Cunningham writes in *The Journal of Pastoral Care,* "A person feels a loneliness and isolation from God because the shame and guilt of wrong doing stores up in one's secret self to the point that one feels self-hatred and seeks to avoid God, the church, and those closest to him or her."[3]

In some cases, those who hide their anger practice passive-aggressive behavior, acting out against God in strange ways that sometimes confuse even them. Without realizing it, they are trying to punish God for letting them down.

A Prescription for Healing

If you find yourself in this situation—with anger hidden under your weariness—what can you do about it? We can't promise any instant cures, but by picking up this book you've already taken a step toward healing. That step is the recognition of your anger at God, or at least *considering* that you might be angry at

God, and a desire to do something about it, or at least to consider doing something about it.

But healing takes time. Your anger won't resolve itself overnight. Be patient; your situation can improve. Let's look at some of the pieces of the healing process:

- ≪ Own up to your honest emotions.
- ≪ Express your anger in healthy ways.
- ≪ Reevaluate the situation that prompted your anger.
- ≪ Understand your own neediness.
- ≪ Reach out for a restored relationship.

Own Up to Your Honest Emotions

Since God already knows your heart, trying to fool him by hiding your true feelings won't work. Just because we don't *say* that we're sad, mad, disappointed, or whatever doesn't mean that God doesn't know. In fact, saying we are happy and fine when we're not doesn't fool him either.

But don't rush right into your anger. The events or perceptions that made you angry have probably sparked a process that has led you through disappointment, feelings of betrayal and abandonment, and a sense of being alone, which may bring sadness, cynicism, and weariness. You now have a stew of emotions that you need to sift through. Don't deny what you feel just because it's not an emotion that others approve of. Claim your feelings.

If you are sad, say so. Let yourself be sad. Do you have a sense of loss? What do you feel you have lost? Have a good cry over these losses. God gave us tears to cleanse our memories. Forget the nonsense that demands nonstop cheeriness. Give yourself permission to mourn.

In the Jewish tradition, when a person dies, he or she is mourned by family and friends for a year. Then the person is mentioned in the synagogue, signaling that the time of mourning is over. Whatever you are feeling sad about, these two aspects are vitally important: the time of mourning and the time to stop mourning. And you can't get to the second without the first. When you have suffered a loss, you *have to* mourn adequately. If you don't let yourself mourn, or if you cut short the mourning process, your body and soul will continue the process in other ways. Only by allowing yourself a sufficient time of mourning can you reach the point where you can stop mourning in a healthy way.

There might be other emotions you need to own up to. We've talked about cynicism. If your anger and sadness have brought you to a point of unharnessed negativity, then say so. Quit hiding behind your cloak of sophistication and admit that sometimes you hate the world and everything in it. When you criticize someone, be sure to add, "But of course I'm always in a bad mood and there's really nothing you could say or do to please me." You would shock them. You might shock yourself. And when you hear yourself saying those words, you might finally realize that it doesn't have to be that way. You might find a way to make peace with some of the provinces of the world around you.

If you're feeling weary of life in general, admit that. Then give yourself a vacation. We're not talking principally about physical exhaustion (though it often manifests itself physically); this is weariness of the soul. Since God is out of the picture, you've had to do everything on your own. Every day you summon your own strength to get you through, and now you don't have much left. Can you get to a point where you pray for help?

Once you accept your feelings of sadness, cynicism, or weariness, you may clear the way again for your angry feelings—and this may frighten you. You've been sweeping this dust under the rug for so long that when you finally remove the rug, the dust bunnies attack! You've been dampening your anger with these "down" feelings, but as you deal with those feelings, you may find a new burst of negative energy.

That's okay.

If you get nothing else from this book, get this: *It's okay to feel angry at God.* "Every real human relationship encompasses moments of tenderness and joy as well as outbursts of irritation and even hatred," notes Sheila Carney.[4] The same holds true for our relationship with God: "Even as we seek to love and serve him we experience moments of indifference, anger, hatred."[5]

In his foreword to a book by Pierre Wolff called *May I Hate God?,* the noted devotional writer Henri Nouwen says:

> I would not be surprised if hostility, anger, resentment, and hatred proved to be the greatest stumbling blocks to our spiritual growth. . . . Our first response to such feelings is to hide them from God in the belief that they have no place in our spiritual life. . . . Our spiritual life then loses strength and power and quickly becomes divorced from the issues that really matter. . . . We can do real harm to ourselves when we approach God selectively and reveal to him only those parts of ourselves that we think he can handle. . . . We have been so victimized by religious and secular taboos against anger and hatred that these emotions usually evoke only shame and guilt. Seldom, if ever, are they expressed in a creative way. But Scripture presents us with a real alternative. In both the Old and New Testaments, it is clear that only by expressing our anger and hatred directly to God will we come to know the fullness of both his love and our freedom.[6]

Again, we can find parallels in human relationships. Conflict and misunderstanding are part of human relationships. People need to learn healthy ways of expressing their hurt and angry feelings openly and honestly to one another in a safe environment that encourages resolution, growth, and healing. The most unhealthy approach to conflict in a marriage or among friends is to ignore it, repress it, and withdraw. Reconciliation begins with honestly coming to terms with our feelings and taking the risk to express our feelings. Communication is the foundation of relationships.

But wait a second! We're talking about God here, not your neighbor, not your spouse. God is supreme Creator of all. Don't we owe him some respect?

Absolutely. But which is more respectful: telling someone how angry you are, or storming out of the house? When you repress your anger at God, it's like walking out of the relationship. You can't discuss the issues when you've turned your back. And you can't deepen your love for God when you're bottling up your feelings.

While the Bible upholds the concept of respect for God, remember again that it has *many* examples of faithful people duking it out with the Almighty. Sarah and Samuel, Jacob and David, Peter and Paul—these people weren't shy about telling the Lord how they really felt. Of the 150 Psalms, 33 are known as *imprecatory,* or cursing, psalms. You may meditate on the quiet assurance of "The Lord is my shepherd" in Psalm 23, but flip back a page and you'll read, "My God, my God, why have you forsaken me?" in Psalm 22.

All of this is consistent with the biblical portrait of a God who is fully present with us, not just high and distant from us—*and that includes his honest expression of emotion toward us.* As Carol Christ concludes,

> Martin Buber has suggested that the enigmatic name of God, usually translated as "I am who I am," might better be translated as "I will be there as I will be there," or even "I will be present (to you) as I will be present (to you)." God did not promise always to express loving feelings to the people, but rather to be fully present with whatever God felt in response to

the situation. Thus, God did not withhold anger when the people broke the covenant but was fully present with angry feelings. . . . Had God repressed anger instead of expressing it, Israel would not have known the living God in the fullness of being. Like any other relation where anger is not expressed, the covenantal relation would have stagnated, gone dead.[7]

"The biblical notion of relationship with a living God implies full presence," notes another scholar. "He does not withhold anger when the people break the covenant, nor does he have any expectation that they will repress their feelings when they think he has broken it. . . . Wesley Baker suggests that the great commandment 'You shall love the LORD your God with all your heart and with all your soul and with all your might' (Deuteronomy 6:5, [NASB]) is a command that we strive for wholeness in all our relationships—a wholeness which encompasses appropriate expressions of anger."[8]

Express Your Anger in Healthy Ways

After you've admitted to yourself that you're angry at God, it's important to express your anger in healthy ways. But how? Anger can certainly be destructive, and that's why many people shy away from it. If the only expressions of anger you've seen have been wildly violent or brazenly disrespectful, you won't trust anger to advance a relationship—especially a relationship with God.

Marie's husband had left her for another woman, and Marie was very angry. She took an ax and went through their house destroying everything that was his—his desk, his golf clubs, his favorite chair. Her children were terrified as they helplessly watched their mother rage out of control destroying their home. What do you think those children learned about anger? It's likely that they learned to fear anger, in others and in themselves.

But anger doesn't have to be like Marie's violent rampage. It can be expressed in controlled, helpful, even therapeutic ways. In fact, anger often helps us understand who we are by calling attention to what's most important to us. In a marriage, properly expressed anger can help the partners understand each other better. We presume that God already knows us perfectly, but our anger can reveal to us our own innermost needs, values, and priorities.

So listen to your anger, but don't believe everything it says. Anger is often based on perceptions that are inadequate or mistaken. Express your anger, but always allow for the possibility that you might be wrong. As Harriet Lerner puts it, "Too often, anger propels us to take positions that we have not thought through carefully enough or that we are not really ready to take. *'Slow down!'* Our anger can be a powerful vehicle for personal growth and change."[9]

The expression of anger has three basic parts: announcing the emotion; presenting the case; and releasing the energy. In the first part, you tell the person that you're angry—*I'm so mad at you!* That, by itself, cannot be argued. The object of your anger may give a thousand reasons why you should not be angry, but he or she cannot deny that you *are.* Yet the mere announcement of anger is difficult for many people, especially when God is the object.

Presenting the case is simply saying *why* you're angry. You explain what the other person did or didn't do to upset you—*You made me wait in that restaurant for two hours and you never called!* The underlying issue is always justice. You feel you have been treated unfairly, and you're laying out the charges. And here's where arguments occur, because you could be wrong. You might be misunderstanding what happened or why, or your sense of justice may be skewed in your favor. If you have put the other person on the defensive, he or she will launch back with a litany of *your* misdeeds and why you deserve the bad treatment you received.

Throughout this process, you are stirring up energy that must be released. Unfortunately, this leads some people to violence, but it doesn't have to. That energy can be rechanneled in any number of ways. Sometimes just the act of shouting at the other person releases enough energy, but sometimes the physical tension is so great that you need to jab at a punching bag or a pillow for a while. You could go running or clean the house—whatever works for you.

Sometimes there's a fourth part to the expression of anger: vengeance. Since we have been treated unfairly, we try to even things out by hurting the other person. Sometimes that means our energy is "released" on the other person's nose. At other times the revenge is more creative: sabotage, slander, that sort of thing. When people say, "I don't get mad, I get even," they're saying they prefer to circumvent the healthy expression of anger.

The healthy expression of anger involves the first three, but never the fourth. Let's restate its parts or elements.

1. The *announcement* is clear and forthright—*I am angry at you!*—not shrouded in dirty looks, snide comments, or other passive-aggressive behavior.

2. The *presentation* becomes an opportunity for communication rather than attack. Your goal is to improve the relationship, helping the other person to understand rather than trying to make him or her feel bad.

3. The *physical energy* is rechanneled in harmless ways.

Now how do we apply this to our anger at God? It's not much of a stretch. First we need to announce to God that we are angry. Sure, he knows this already, but maybe you don't. By announcing it, you are claiming your emotions, giving yourself permission to feel what you feel.

In the second part, we need to explain *why* we're angry at God. As with human relationships, we need to make this a time of communication rather than attack. Present your case, but also listen for any responses God might have. If your thoughts are tumbling out too quickly, try writing God a letter explaining your feelings. If you're having a hard time knowing what to say or write, pull out one of those psalms of complaint and use that as a model.

One way of listening for God's response might be to read some of the biblical passages where God communicated with those who expressed anger. Or you might just be quiet for a while and tune in to God's "gentle whisper." Or perhaps a wise friend or counselor can help you through this. But be careful to find one who won't scold you for expressing your anger at God. Not everyone realizes how important this is.

Finally, release that energy. Scream. Shout at God. Cry. Punch something (not someone). Do situps. Hurl a tennis ball against your garage door. Ride a bike uphill. (Be careful about driving a car, though.)

My (Michele's) friend Karen was grieving the death of her husband. He had died of cancer, and her tears never seemed to stop flowing. Yet anger seemed to be hidden underneath the tears. Karen realized she needed to get her anger out. After discussing a variety of options, she chose her venting strategy.

We went shopping in thrift shops for cheap, ugly dishes. At the third store we found the perfect set: a large box of olive green and brown dishes for under ten dollars. Karen proudly took her find to the register and smiled as the clerk began to wrap the dishes carefully.

"That won't be necessary," Karen told the clerk.

"But, my dear," the clerk replied, "they might chip or break."

Karen and I both laughed, knowing the fate of the dishes. That was the whole idea.

Back at Karen's home, we went out into the woods behind her house with the box of old dishes. Karen gingerly hurled the first one at a tree, smashing the plate. "I hate cancer!" she yelled, and a sense of relief came over her. She quickly reached for another. "God, why did he have to die?" Karen hurled plate after plate into the tree as she shouted her questions at God. "I'm mad at you, God, for leaving me all alone now. I don't understand any of this and I don't like it!"

Soon the plates were demolished, but Karen's relationship with God was stronger. She had thrown her anger at God with all the energy she could muster, and now she was ready to move on.

The three parts of expressing anger are not necessarily sequential. You can release, announce, and explain all at once, as Karen did in the woods behind her home. In fact, if you normally pray with hands folded and eyes closed, you might want to take your prayer out for some exercise. Pray as you run or walk or play. Get those feelings out spiritually, emotionally, and physically at the same time.

Reevaluate the Situation
That Prompted Your Anger

After admitting your anger and expressing it, you need to reevaluate the situation that prompted your anger. As you listen for God's response, you may discover that your anger at God was based on a misunderstanding. In Psalm 73, the writer complains about injustice for sixteen verses, "till I entered the sanctuary of God; then I understood." But if that happens, it doesn't mean you were wrong to feel angry or to express your anger. That's how you honestly felt, and it would be wrong to deny it. Even if there was a misunderstanding, your anger would have succeeded in raising an issue that needed clarification. Because you honestly expressed your anger to God, rather than letting negative feelings drive you away, you were able to receive God's grace through a new perspective.

Now that you've opened up lines of communication with God, you'll be in a better position to learn who God really is, as opposed to one of those false images of who you think God is or who you think he's supposed to be. You're listening now for the truth.

Understand Your Own Neediness

After reevaluating the situation, you might need to understand your own neediness. Anger has a way of puffing us up. A guy in a bar fight announces, "You don't want to mess with me. They used to call me the Bully of Baker Street." He fails to mention that the only other residents of Baker Street were seven years old.

When we're angry, we start totaling up the injustices we have experienced, but our judgment is easily skewed. Every sidelong glance, every less-than-flattering comment, every imagined snub gets thrown into the mix. We feel that we haven't gotten what we deserve, but perhaps we've inflated our own importance. Perhaps we're not as deserving as we think.

In a marriage, this inflation creates what we call the *45 percent effect.* When a marriage gets in trouble, each partner starts scrupulously counting up all the favors done for the other partner. Both of them think they're putting 50 percent of the effort into the relationship, but they're both overestimating their contribution. They're both actually investing only 45 percent of the effort needed to make the marriage work, which of course creates a substantial gap. They overestimate what they deserve and they underestimate what they receive.

The same thing can happen in our relationship with God. We might start comparing ourselves with other people. "I work just as hard as he does. Why don't I get my fair share?" Of course, even if we're counting properly, such comparisons are always irrelevant. God is like the landowner in Jesus' parable who agreed to pay his workers "whatever is right." He has separate "contracts" with each of us.

But in our angry moments we still assume that God owes us more than he's provided. Or when something bad happens, we moan, "What did I do to deserve this?" We build our houses on a flood plain and then scold God when the river rises. God might very well respond, "What *didn't* you do to deserve this?" We are flawed people who often make bad choices. We may never know how often he has rescued us from negative consequences but we still get upset when he doesn't.

So as you take a new look at the events that have prompted your anger, be sure to let some air out of your ego. Try to get a realistic view of your own role in these events and your own standing with God. Grab some humility once again.

But please understand that this is a later step in the process. Some people are so frantic about appearing humble before God that they never reveal their true feelings. They theologize first, and that keeps them from emotionalizing. "Who am I to question God?" they proclaim. "I am just a lowly sinner. I have no right to express feelings of anger."

Well, yes and no. We are all "lowly sinners," but God has given us the right to express our feelings of anger. We must unleash our honest emotions in healthy ways in order to restore equilibrium in our relationships.

Reach Out for a Restored Relationship

Finally, after we puncture the puffed-up balloon of our self-importance, we need to reach out for a restored relationship. Anger can unite or divide people. We need to reconnect after our expressions of anger.

Once again, we can learn from human relationships. "The best thing about having a fight in a marriage," one woman told us, arm in arm with her husband, "is making up." And it's true. When couples know how to fight, they can cleanse a relationship. They identify their needs, set new ground rules, and actually express their passionate commitment to the relationship. After the emotions cool down and apologies are made, a couple can experience a new togetherness.

In a relationship with God, the honest expression of anger can result in a clearer sense of that relationship. Who are you? Who is God to you? What can you expect? What can he expect of you? The commitment can reach a new level if you let it.

Unfortunately, many people feel ashamed after getting mad at God. Like Adam and Eve, they hide in the bushes when God comes out for his daily walk with them. God is ready to take the next step in the relationship, but they are fearful. Don't let that happen to you. The best thing about having a fight with God is making up.

CHAPTER FIVE

MASTER OF DISGUISE

A knock at the door. A friend urging escape. And the young girl, now about sixteen, was whisked away to a new life. A small group of people made the escape from Constantinople, traveling through the mountains in hopes of finding freedom and safety. The husband of Helen's cousin was in the Turkish army, and he had orchestrated this rescue to bring his captive wife back home. Helen was fortunate to be included.

With hearts racing, they left the city that night and journeyed quickly through the winter snow. Helen's cousin rode on the horse her husband had provided for her. The others walked.

But Helen was having trouble keeping up. It was a long and difficult journey by foot through the snow. The mountains were steep and treacherous. She had difficulty breathing and had to stop at regular intervals. It was cold, very cold, and the snow had begun to fall again. With the quick getaway, Helen had been unable to pack extra clothing. Now her hands and feet were growing numb. She didn't think she could walk much farther.

Filled with compassion, her cousin got down from her horse and let Helen ride. Poor Helen was too weak even to sit on the horse and had to be tied on. Helen would probably have died along the way if it weren't for this act of kindness. The group traveled on.

The next day, as they moved along the snow-covered mountain trail, Helen's cousin took a false step into a snowdrift that covered a crevasse. She fell far into the snow. The others tried to save her, but couldn't. They had to leave her there to die.

Helen always felt guilty about that. The woman had essentially given her life for Helen, offering her mount to the struggling girl. *That should be me dead in the snow,* Helen thought as she traveled on. They finally reached their destination and the soldier came out to greet his wife, only to find young Helen riding in her place. In his grief, he blamed the girl for his wife's death. Still, he took her in for a short time until he was able to send her to an orphanage in another town.

The Turks had set up orphanages for Armenian children to teach them Turkish culture and the Muslim religion. This was another way to wipe out the Armenian race. As Helen settled into this new home, she knew she would be provided for, but she also knew she would lose all links to her past life.

She had physical problems as well. Her hands were seriously frostbitten, and gangrene could set in. At the orphanage, a visiting doctor examined Helen and made plans to amputate at least one if not both of her hands the next day. Fear and terror once again gripped her. The headstrong Helen couldn't imagine life without her hands. That night, she ran away from the orphanage.

Racing blindly into the night, she took a chance and knocked on a door, seeking refuge. She didn't know what fate awaited her. Turkish families giving aid to Armenians could be killed. Still, desperate to escape, she knocked. The door was answered by a kind Turkish couple who took her in. This couple regularly welcomed travelers. It so happened that, while Helen was staying there, a caravan driver stopped at the same house. He noticed her infected hands and offered her a salve he used for frostbite. Whipping up a strange concoction, the man rubbed it on her deadened hands.

Over the next few days, her hands healed. She regained feeling. Amputation would not be necessary after all.

By this time, the world had become more aware of the Armenians' plight, and several international and missionary agencies were offering aid. In addition to the Turkish orphanages assimilating Armenian children as Turks, these agencies established other centers where children could be reunited with living family members. And so, after experiencing unexpected Turkish hospitality, Helen wound up in an internationally run orphanage, where she learned that her mother had survived the death march and was living in Bulgaria. Now Helen had the option to go to Bulgaria and start a new life there with her mother.

But Helen said no. She was filled with rage toward her mother. Everything that had happened to their family was because of her mother's refusal to renounce her God. Her father had not wanted them to leave. He was willing to renounce the Christian God. But her mother had made him feel guilty. And look where standing up for God had gotten them! Yes, it was all her mother's fault. And after all that, Helen's mother was *still* a Christian, and a cheerful one at that. All through the desert, her mother Anna had kept praying, and Helen couldn't stand it. She blamed God for all this misfortune, and her mother was God's representative on earth. Besides that, she still feared that the Turkish officer would come looking for her. Even Bulgaria wasn't far enough away. No, she would not join her mother there. She wanted to go to America.

But emigration to the United States wouldn't be easy. Ocean passage was expensive, and you had to have an American sponsor to welcome you. One of the best ways for adolescent girls to make the move was participation in a "picture bride" program. Armenian organizations would gather photos of girls wanting to come to America and publish them in booklets that were distributed to Armenian men already in America. If a man saw someone he might want to marry, he could start up a correspondence with her through the sponsoring organization. If all went well, he could send money for the trip and meet the girl at Ellis Island.

In the orphanage, Helen and a friend decided to sign up for the program. Her friend was quite an attractive young woman but Helen wasn't. The friend quickly got a response from Michael Jamgochian, a man from Pennsylvania, and began exchanging photos and letters. Helen waited in vain to find a sponsor.

Eventually, her friend received money from Michael to pay for her trip, but at the last minute she decided not to go. Helen leapt at the opportunity, taking the money and going to America in her friend's place.

After a long and uncomfortable journey, Helen finally saw the Statue of Liberty—"the Lady," she called her. At Ellis Island she gave her friend's name and waited to be introduced to the man who had paid her passage. But when Michael saw Helen instead of his picture bride, he knew he'd been duped. This wasn't the wife he wanted. He wouldn't accept her.

Having traveled halfway around the world, Helen was alone again. She stood there on the dock, rejected by her new country, just as she had been rejected by God. What could she do? She knew no one else in America. She cried out desperately for help. "No, you mustn't send me back. I won't go! I can't go back there!" Helen's pleas were falling on deaf ears. Michael Jamgochian stood firm in his refusal.

An Armenian minister was there, though, making connections for the new arrivals. Fluent in the Armenian language, he was able to translate between the new arrivals and some of the second- or third-generation Armenian-Americans who no longer knew their people's tongue. Hearing Helen's tirade, he rushed to see what was wrong. Then he tried to intercede with Michael on Helen's behalf. But Michael and his family staunchly refused to take her in. He had been cheated by her; he certainly wouldn't marry her.

Still, Helen loudly announced that she was not going back to Turkey, never. She was here in America and she would stay. But unless she had a sponsor, American officials wouldn't let her into the country. She'd remain on Ellis Island until this matter was resolved. No matter what, the headstrong, desperate seventeen-year-old vowed she wouldn't budge from this country.

Reluctantly, the minister put his arm around the obstinate girl. "I'll sponsor you, my child," he said.

Where Is He?

Just when things seemed to get better for Helen, they got worse. Plucked from the desert, she became a slave to a Turkish officer. Saved from slavery, she was forced on a difficult march that froze her hands. And just when fortune started to smile, sending her to America in place of her friend, she was rejected again and left all alone.

You might have similar ups and downs in your life—a promising marriage that fell apart, a job opportunity that vanished, a physical ailment that kept you from doing what you wanted. Just when hope starts to bloom, it gets trampled on.

Where is God when you need him?

Well, he's there when the cousin knocks at the door with a way of escape. He's there in the woman who gives her horse—and her life—for the needy child. He appears as a mysterious caravan driver with a healing balm, as a beautiful friend who decides not to take a boat ride, and as a minister on a New York dock. Helen might have every reason to feel rejected by God, except for his messengers.

"Do not fear," the Lord said to Israel, "for I am with you" (Isaiah 41:10). That's his calling card: that he is with us . . . even when he doesn't seem to be.

The story is told of a talented boy who won the lead in his class play. We'll call him Ricky. His mother had studied acting herself, so she was eager to help her son do well. She went to every rehearsal and took notes on his work. At home, she would review his efforts and help him improve.

But a few days before the performance, Ricky's teacher called his mother. "I know you mean well," the teacher said, "but we think you're hindering Ricky's performance. He seems to hold back when you're there, as if he's afraid to do something you don't like. We're wondering if you could stay away from the remaining rehearsals and see if that helps any."

The mother was upset, but willing to help, so she skipped the next few rehearsals. Still, she couldn't resist calling the teacher for a progress report. "I know it's hard for you," the teacher said, "but Ricky's doing much better on stage. He's much more creative. It's good that you're not there." It was indeed difficult for the mother to stay away, but she saw the value in it. Ricky needed to do this play on his own, in his own way.

The performance night came, and Ricky did very well. Still, he left the stage crying. When he got home, he yelled at his mother, "Why weren't you there? All the other kids' parents were there, but not you. There was even a bag lady who came in off the street and sat in the back row. *She* gave me a standing ovation, but you weren't even there to see it. I thought you loved me." Then he collapsed in tears.

The mother gathered the boy into her arms and said, "I do love you, Ricky, and you did a beautiful job in the play." Ricky pulled away from her and gave her a puzzled, hurt look. "You see," she explained, "I was that bag lady."

It turns out that God is a master of disguise. He is there for us, even when we don't recognize him. This has to do with some of the imagery we've already discussed. When we're looking for God in the wind, earthquake, or fire, we can easily ignore the gentle whisper in our ear. If we expect God to come thundering into our lives with a fifteen-point plan for personal renewal, we can dismiss the advice he gives us through our brother-in-law or minister.

You may have heard the story of the man whose town was being flooded. He heard a radio report urging evacuation, but he stayed put. "God will keep me from harm," he figured. As the floodwaters rose, a neighbor came by in a rowboat, offering to ferry him out of danger. "No, no," he responded. "God will keep me from harm." Finally, the man was perched on a small patch of his roof, with water all around him, when he heard a helicopter hovering above. A loudspeaker crackled, "We're throwing down a rope! Climb on!" But he waved his arms and hollered, "No, thanks, God will keep me from harm!"

The water continued to rise and finally the man drowned.

In heaven, he stormed past St. Peter and strode up to God's throne in a huff. "I trusted you to protect me, Lord. Where were you?"

And God replied, "I sent you the radio report, the rowboat, and the helicopter. What more did you want?"

God is active in the world around us, offering guidance, help, and comfort. We don't always know he's the one helping us. For some reason, he likes it that way. There is much wisdom in the bumper sticker that says, "Coincidence is when God chooses to act anonymously."

In the Bible we get glimpses of him in the strangers who visit the aged Abraham and Sarah with a surprise birth announcement; in the mysterious man who wrestles with Jacob the night before he reunites with his murderous brother; in the fourth man who stands unsinged in the fiery furnace with Daniel's faithful friends. We see him working quietly behind the scenes to turn evil plans to his good purposes. Prince Haman's pride gets him hanged on his own gallows, while Esther saves her people from his holocaust. As a prince of Egypt, Joseph surprises the brothers who had sold him as a slave. "You meant it for evil," he tells them, "but God meant it for good." As Joseph had languished in prison, the gears of God's purposes were already quietly turning.

We can go months, even years, without hearing a clear word from him, but that doesn't mean he's gone on vacation. He's just working undercover.

You might have laughed at the silly spy sitcom *Get Smart,* as Max would go to the corner mailbox and find a federal agent inside. But that's the idea God gives us of his own presence, watching over us but also giving us some leeway. He's on every corner, behind that lamppost, balanced on that building ledge— around us, but not in our faces.

He's like a father teaching a child to ride a bike. For a while the father holds the handlebars and runs alongside. Then he holds the back of the seat or the rear fender as the child steers. Finally he lets go, and the child rides free. Imagine a little girl who rides half a block on her own and then crashes. Holding her skinned knee, she cries out to her father, "Where were you when I needed you?"

The answer is, "I was there, but I had to let go. That's the whole idea." You wouldn't want to see a fifteen-year-old riding her bike on her paper route with Dad dutifully running alongside, holding her up. He has to let go. And if we learn anything from the history of humanity and the whole problem of evil, it's that freedom is very, very important to God. Sometimes he has to let go.

God and Suffering

God also sits with us in our suffering. The idea of a suffering God is outrageous to some, but that's how he often portrays himself in the Old and New Testaments. Why should the Creator of all, the King of the Universe, the Lord of Lords, ever have to feel pain of any kind? We don't know. Maybe it's out of love for his creatures.

Jilted Lover

The Old Testament is filled with images of God as a jilted lover. The first commandment, "You shall have no other gods before me," is a kind of marriage contract. "Forsaking all others," God's people should follow the one who loves them. But God's beloved ones are promiscuous, and this causes him great pain.

We see it most clearly in the story of the prophet Hosea, whose life became an object lesson for the Lord he served. God told Hosea to marry a prostitute. (Some think she became a prostitute *after* the wedding, but no matter.) In any case, despite Hosea's love and commitment, his wife ran after other lovers. Hosea would give her gifts, but she would assume her other lovers had sent them. She bore two children, and Hosea never seemed quite sure they were his. (He named one of them "Not mine," but later changed it to "Mine.") At one point, following God's instructions, Hosea went and bought his wife back from her brothel.

In this soap opera, Hosea was playing the role of God, as he made clear in the biblical book he wrote. God had established a relationship with his people, Israel. They had been unfaithful, following after other gods—especially the local sky-god, Baal. God sent them rain and crops and bounty, but they assumed it was Baal lavishing these gifts upon them. He was deeply hurt by their infidelity.

"What can I do with you, Ephraim?" God moaned, using his nickname for the nation of Israel. "Your love is like the morning mist, like the early dew that disappears" (Hosea 6:4). Then he says,

> *"I long to redeem them*
> *but they speak lies against me.*
> *They do not cry out to me from their hearts*
> *but wail upon their beds."* (7:13-14)

Later, we get a slightly different picture that's both tender and devastating: God as the parent of a toddler.

"When Israel was a child, I loved him . . .
But the more I called Israel,
the further they went from me.
They sacrificed to the Baals
and they burned incense to images.
It was I who taught Ephraim to walk,
taking them by the arms;
but they did not realize
it was I who healed them." (11:1-3)

Why is God suffering? Because he has put his heart in the hands of his creatures and they have broken it.

In 1936 the world gasped as the king of England abdicated his throne to marry an American divorcée. How many other powerful, talented, brilliant people have put themselves and all they had in the hands of someone they loved? It's an old story—love conquers power. And somehow, God's supreme love makes him dote on the creatures he fashioned from the dust of the earth, humanity.

That doesn't mean he can't get tough. Sometimes the pain of his love seems to drive him to acts of punishment. Just before some of the tender cooing we quoted, he says,

"I killed you with the words of my mouth;
my judgments flashed like lightning upon you." (6:5)

And he cries,

"Woe to them,
because they have strayed from me!
Destruction to them,
because they have rebelled against me!" (7:13)

But the purpose of all this is love. A moment later he's rethinking his harshness.

> *"How can I give you up, Ephraim?*
> *How can I hand you over, Israel?. . .*
> *My heart is changed within me;*
> *all my compassion is aroused.*
> *I will not carry out my fierce anger."* (11:8-9)

And once again he is madly in love with his precious people, allowing them to hold the key to his heart.

This is a stunning portrait of God. We understand the tortured emotions of being loved and not loved, of being totally devoted to someone who toys with our affections. We've been there. The surprising thing is that God has been there, too.

Some scholars dismiss this as an anthropomorphism — Hosea's attempt to depict God as a man like himself, subject to the same passions. That might make sense if this were an isolated example, but the Bible keeps returning to this theme. Jeremiah hears God saying, "Return, faithless people . . . for I am your husband" (3:14). The prophet Ezekiel picks up the theme as well. G. K. Chesterton felt the central idea of the Old Testament was the loneliness of God.

We even catch a whiff of it back in Eden, as God comes out to walk with Adam and Eve when they've sinned and gone into hiding. "Where are you?" he cries (Genesis 3:9). The tragedy of sin had changed everything, but that's when God begins to hatch his plot to win back his creatures' love.

Suffering Servant

We also see God in the image of the suffering servant. The prophet Isaiah waxed eloquent on this theme. At first we see the picture of a king who will lead the world into a new era:

> *"Here is my servant, whom I uphold,*
> *my chosen one in whom I delight;*
> *I will put my Spirit on him*
> *and he will bring justice to the nations."* (Isaiah 42:1)

But the story takes a few twists and turns along the way. In Isaiah 53:3 we read,

> *He was despised and rejected by men,*
> *a man of sorrows, and familiar with suffering.*
> *Like one from whom men hide their faces*
> *he was despised, and we esteemed him not.*

The text goes on to describe his being stricken, smitten, afflicted, pierced, crushed, punished, wounded, oppressed, and led like a lamb to the slaughter.

One traditional Jewish interpretation sees the servant as a personification of Israel, bearing the sin of the world on her wounded back. But the early Christians quickly found this to be a prophecy about Jesus, the Messiah, who would "bring justice to the nations" by suffering for the world's sin: "and the LORD has laid on him the iniquity of us all" (Isaiah 53:6).

This fit in with Jesus' description of himself as one who "did not come to be served, but to serve, and to give his life as a ransom for many" (Matthew 20:28). Christian teaching puts God right beside us in our suffering, in the person of Christ. He doesn't expect us to endure anything he hasn't gone through already. The book of Hebrews depicts Jesus as a high priest who brings us into the Father's presence: "For we do not have a high priest who is unable to sympathize with our weaknesses, but we have one who has been tempted in every way, just as we are" (4:15). As a result, we can approach God's throne "with confidence, so that we may receive mercy and find grace to help us in our time of need" (4:16).

In a church drama I (Randy) wrote, three very different people cry out to God in their need. A teenage girl complains that her mother has no clue about her goals and aspirations: "You don't know what it's like to have a mother who just seems to have no clue about what you should be doing! Well, yeah, there was that time at the temple. You were, what? Twelve?. . . But apart from that, you have no idea what it's like!" A furious businessman rails at God for letting his friend grab the promotion that *he* had been counting on: "Do you have any idea how it feels to be betrayed by one of your closest friends? To invest your time and friendship and have them sell you out? Oh, yeah. Maybe you do." An older woman ponders an upcoming surgery, wondering how long she'll have to live, and she asks God, "Do you understand how it feels to be facing death, but to want so very much to live? Oh, you do, don't you?"[1]

Yes, he knows. He has been there, done that. He's no stranger to suffering.

That doesn't make everything all better. If you're ailing in the hospital, it's nice to know that Jesus is in the next bed, but it doesn't stop the pain. Still, it shows us how important suffering is in God's eyes. If he has the power to avoid suffering but chooses to go through it, he must have good reason to do so. We may never know the reason entirely, but it must be important.

And that sense of purpose may be enough to lift us from despair to acceptance. Viktor Frankl, who suffered in Nazi concentration camps, developed a concept he called *logotherapy.* Basically, the theory asserts that a person can get through difficult times if he or she has a sense of purpose in the suffering. According to logotherapy, if we have a reason *(logos)* to survive, we can bear the suffering. "Suffering ceases to be suffering in some way," said Frankl, "at the moment it finds a meaning."[2]

That's the emotional battleground for many in turmoil. The suffering seems so random, so senseless—how could it have any purpose at all? *Why did that drunk driver have to veer into my lane?* If God is far away from us, we can blame him for being wicked, weak, or apathetic. But when we understand that he suffers with us, we can assume there is some good to be found amid the evil. Perhaps our pain is a cauldron for some sort of divine alchemy. Perhaps we can grow to understand him better as we share our suffering with him. That may be reason enough to get us through.

The Little Miracles

Sometimes God works miracles for us. Sometimes he doesn't. These miracles can be wonderful reminders of his presence—but they can also be tantalizingly incomplete. It's amazing that God can send a caravan driver to heal Helen's hands from frostbite. It's not hard to think of this man as an angel who suddenly appeared to work this wonder and then disappeared just as quickly. But if God cared so much about Helen's hands, why did he let them get frostbitten in the first place? Why did he allow the horrendous circumstances that put her on that snow-laden trail? Why didn't he save her father or brother or sisters from death?

The skeptics have a point. When you start throwing around miracles as examples of God's love and power, you also need to consider the miracles that he *doesn't* perform. Does that mean he lacks power or love? When you're already nursing a grudge against God, such displays can backfire. You might feel as if God is taunting you, doing some healing but not enough. You might get even angrier—or you might prefer to ignore the miracles altogether.

Helen took the latter path. To a person of faith, several events in her story seem to be obvious examples of God's handiwork. But for decades afterward, Helen refused to see this. She felt guilty, not grateful, for the woman who let her ride on the horse and later died. She felt lucky that the Turkish family took her in and lucky that the caravan driver happened to stop by. She felt entitled to the sponsorship by the Armenian minister after she had crossed an ocean to find a new life in America. Miracles? Not to her.

But if you accept these events as miracles, you're stuck with a crucial question. Why some and not all? Why heal the hands and not her whole history?

The Why of Miracles

First, let's consider why God works miracles. In general, as you look through the Bible and history, there seem to be three major reasons for miracles:

- ⊰ Demonstrations of God's presence, love, or power
- ⊰ Healing
- ⊰ Guidance

Miracles, by definition, are strange phenomena. They often consist of the overturning of some physical law of nature or a departure from the regular course of events. Jesus tells servants to pour water into big stone pots and suddenly it becomes wine. Paul is bitten by a poisonous viper but isn't affected. Daniel spends the night with carnivorous lions and emerges uneaten. If you try really hard, you might come up with natural explanations for these events, but the simplest explanation—and the one adopted by people on the scene in each case—is that the laws of nature were overturned by a force greater than nature. And so each of these occurrences testified to the power of God as well as God's connection to the person involved. King Darius decreed that Daniel's God was the true God. The citizens of Malta understood that Paul had divine power (in fact, they misunderstood and thought that *he* was a god). And Jesus' miracles—water to wine, healings, walking on water, calming storms—confirmed that he was on a mission from God. As Peter preached in his first sermon, "Jesus of Nazareth was a man accredited by God to you by miracles, wonders and signs, which God did among you through him" (Acts 2:22).

Miracles serve as demonstrations that God is present with a person, that God cares for a person, or that God has power over nature. They're God's way of showing his character. Even today, missionaries report that in certain cultures, miracles convince the locals that the God of the missionaries is someone to be reckoned with.

God is also a healer, and sometimes he works quiet miracles that make a person whole. When the psalmist praises the Lord for "all his benefits," he lists among those benefits that the Lord "forgives all your sins and heals all your diseases" (Psalm 103:3). Does God really heal *all* diseases, or is that just poetic license? Well, maybe the psalmist is getting carried away. . . or maybe he's talking about a healing process that will last through eternity, on into the next world. The point is that God likes wholeness — spiritually and physically — and that even nowadays he sometimes overturns the regular course of nature to defeat a disease.

Sometimes God works miracles to provide guidance as he did in Numbers 22 with Balaam and his talking donkey. Balaam was headed where God didn't want him to go, so God sent an angel to stand in the way. Balaam didn't see the angel, but the donkey did. (We don't always notice God's guiding miracles at first. Sometimes he has to work harder to get our attention.)

In Helen's case, the series of events that got her to America seem to be guiding miracles, although she didn't realize it at the time. Yes, you might credit her own tenacity, but there were other factors beyond her control that helped make it happen.

Why Not Fix Everything?

All right, then. God works miracles for various reasons. But why does he insist on working these minor miracles instead of the major ones that keep us from suffering?

Think of a faithful Christian man named Robertson McQuilkin, who gave up his job as the president of a college to care for his wife, Muriel, who suffered from Alzheimer's disease. He tells of one incident when they were staying at a beachfront motel and she was relaxing on the beach while he was in the room, watching her through the window. She sometimes became disoriented and wandered off, so he had learned to keep an eye on her. On this day, suddenly he looked up and she was gone. Frantically he searched, running up and down the beach. "Finally," he says, "exhausted and helpless, I returned to our room—only to discover Muriel! Seems some 'nice young man' had offered her a ride home. He drove down the beach highway until she spotted our motel. Spotted our motel? In that string of look-alikes, even I had difficulty spotting ours."

He was delighted and relieved to have his wife back safely, but the whole incident seemed strange. How could Muriel, in her condition, recognize the place? And who was this "nice young man" who helped her? "I believe in guardian angels," McQuilkin writes. Muriel's children suggested that God had assigned her a whole platoon.[3]

That's a sweet story of God's protection, but we can already hear the skeptics objecting: "Why does God bring her back to the hotel but doesn't cure her disease? If he's so concerned about her safety, why doesn't God just help her think more clearly?"

It's a good question, and we're not sure we can explain it fully, but we'd like to offer the following four ideas:

- Already but not yet
- Reality therapy
- Playing hard to get
- The nature of things

Already but Not Yet

God has great plans for this world, but he's decided to wait a while to fulfill them. In the parable we've already mentioned, the landowner lets the weeds grow with the wheat until the harvest. Things may seem bleak now, but the harvest is coming. And still God sprinkles some of his benefits upon the earth even now, in anticipation of future redemption. As a mother making brownies lets a child lick the spatula, so God gives us a taste of what's to come. He doesn't heal all our diseases yet, but he heals some.

In fact, when we pray, "Thy kingdom come," that's what we're praying for: that God would bring some of his future blessings into our lives today. Robertson McQuilkin knows that his wife will be thinking clearly when she's finally in God's kingdom, but in the meantime he's grateful for the safety God provides them.

Some theologians talk about this concept as *already but not yet*. That's where we live: already receiving some of the blessings of God's redemption, but still longing for its fullness. With this in mind, we can be thankful for the minor miracles and be patient as we await the major ones.

Reality Therapy

My (Michele's) son Duane was late for school. He had shrugged off several parental reminders, and when he was finally ready, he had missed the bus.

"Please, Mom, please drive me," the six-year-old pleaded. "If you don't, I'll be late."

"I know," I responded. "You didn't get ready on time today."

"Come on, Mom! We've got to go *now*!"

I could have left for work right away, and Duane's school was only a five-minute drive from our house, but what would he learn if I helped him out of this jam? He would learn that it wasn't really important to meet the bus schedule, because Mom is always there to help you out. But Mom decided not to be so cooperative.

"You'll have to wait for me to get ready now," I said as he steamed. "I have to get dressed and finish my breakfast."

I did give my son a ride that morning, but intentionally dallied a bit so he would be a few minutes late to school. It wasn't that big a deal, but he had to sign in at the principal's office. A certain number of late arrivals would result in some school discipline.

This is a perfect example of what psychologist Kevin Leman calls *reality discipline,* which is a parenting spinoff of a counseling method known as *reality therapy.*[4] It's a very pragmatic approach to behavior.

In an old Marx Brothers routine, a patient says to a doctor, "It hurts when I do that." The doctor replies, "Then don't do that." That's the idea behind reality therapy. The question repeatedly asked by reality therapists is this: "Is what you are doing getting you what you want?" Our actions have consequences. If you're doing things that have bad consequences for you, stop doing those things. The counselor's job is to help you see a cause/effect relationship and then figure out how to stop the undesirable, ineffective behavior.

Now what if someone steps in to shield you from the bad consequences of your behavior? Does that help you? Maybe in the short term, but not overall. It actually keeps you from experiencing the cause/effect relationship. You learn that your behavior isn't so bad after all.

This is the classic situation of the codependent spouse of an alcoholic or other addict. Such a person *enables* the addictive behavior by protecting the addict from the consequences, even though he or she is just trying to help. If I (Michele) had driven Duane to school on time, I would have been enabling his morning sluggishness. By protecting him from a negative consequence, I would have encouraged more negative behavior in the future—resulting in more negative consequences.

Now we're considering the question of God's miracles on our behalf. Why does he so often work little miracles instead of big ones? This reality therapy answer doesn't work in every case, but it may be the solution for you. You see, sometimes the misfortunes we complain about are at least partially the results of our own behavior. Even when the connection isn't immediately obvious, we often set in motion certain consequences that rebound to hurt us.

Let's say Rachel takes a higher-paying executive job in a different part of the country, so she leaves her social network behind—friends, family, church, community organizations. The new job demands longer hours, and soon she's miserable. She gets home late to her lonely apartment every night, with no friends around to do anything with. "Why, Lord, why did you bring me out here? Why is my life so awful? Help me out here, please!" she laments.

When things start going downhill, we cry out to God to help us . . . and sometimes he does. In Rachel's case, maybe the cleaning lady at her office stops in one night and says a kind word, striking up a conversation that helps Rachel feel better. This isn't the kind of friendship she wanted, not the answer to prayer she expected, but it helps her out of the worst of her loneliness.

What's going on here? Why does God ease her loneliness only a little bit, not a lot? Well, we can't really read God's mind, but we've made up this hypothetical situation, so let's consider it.

Rachel made a decision based on money and vocational advancement. She decided to put her closest relationships in second place in order to move forward in her career. Of course, this is not a grossly immoral choice—hundreds of people do it every day—but her choice still has consequences. So when Rachel suffers from loneliness, we might say she has brought at least some of it on herself. She might cry out to God for relief, and he might provide some, but he also might use reality therapy. He might allow her to experience some of the consequences of her choices, even though he lovingly keeps her from total despair. All because he wants her to understand the importance of community—how her own values have created her present unhappiness.

And then there is Steve, who had a hard time saying no. The people around him knew that, so when they needed something, guess who they went looking for? A ride home? Sure. A loan? No problem. Take over your project at work? Love to. As a result, Steve always seemed to find himself buried under a pile of things to do. And at the top of his list were always the requests of others. He never seemed to be able to get to the tasks that he really wanted to do.

Burdened, frustrated, and overwhelmed, Steve prayed, "God, give me the strength to do all the things I have to do!" He prayed repeatedly but God seemed absent. He never did get the strength to do all that he had on his endlessly growing list of things to do. Was God ignoring Steve's need? Not necessarily. If Steve suddenly had superhuman strength to wipe his slate clean, he wouldn't ever have to look at the cause of his predicament—his inability to set boundaries and say no. Perhaps God was using reality therapy, allowing Steve to experience the consequences of his choices in order to help him grow.

"God is more interested in our faith than in our pleasure," writes Philip Yancey.[5] He wants us to learn and grow through our experiences, just as I (Michele) want my son to learn punctuality. I offer him a little help by driving him to school just a little late, but I don't perform the big miracle of undoing his lateness by driving him to school on time. God often does the same sort of thing for us.

Playing Hard to Get

Josie loves Jack, and she tells him every chance she gets. She thinks about him night and day, sends him gifts and cards, and dreams of marrying him someday. When he calls, she drops everything to talk to him.

Jack is fond of Josie, but not terribly excited about her. He doesn't have to be. She is eternally his, no matter how he treats her, so he doesn't have to try very hard to keep her happy. Yes, he takes her for granted because, well, she *is* granted.

Until she drops some hints about her old friend Raoul coming to town. As much as she'd love to spend Friday night with Jack, she says, she has to show Raoul around. Then she calls to break her Saturday plans with Jack—Raoul is still in town and wants to see the art museum with her.

Jack is beginning to think, *Hmm—I didn't know she liked art.* But then there are a lot of things Jack doesn't know about Josie, including the fact that Raoul is a figment of her imagination. She just read an article in *Mademoiselle* about playing hard to get. When Jack calls her on Monday, she doesn't return the call. He sees her briefly on Wednesday, but she seems preoccupied. She answers his call on Friday, just to say she's busy packing for a weekend trip—she won't say where she's going.

Soon Jack is calling twice a day, sending flowers, begging Josie to see him again: "Maybe I'm not as exotic as Raoul, but I really care about you. I'll do anything for you, Josie." She stifles a laugh—the magazine's plan has worked.

Do we dare compare God's actions to such an adolescent romance? Perhaps. It makes sense that God might play hard to get when we're taking him for granted.

Let's start with the fact that God deeply wants us to choose him. That's what got us into this whole "problem of evil" to begin with, isn't it? He gave us freedom to choose good or evil, to please him or hurt him, to love him or not. He could have denied us freedom, and we would always have followed his will and performed the right actions, like robots. But would the concept of "right" mean anything if we didn't have the power to choose between right and wrong?

Instead, he allowed us to choose whether we would love him, all the while proclaiming his undying love for us. Like Hosea, he goes so far as to dote on an unfaithful wife. Our behavior offends him, but he loves us anyway. He still wants a relationship with us.

We can begin to take that for granted. We count on what Dietrich Bonhoeffer called "cheap grace"—the easy forgiveness of our sins. We can live any way we want; we know God will be there for us.

But through the centuries, saints and theologians have noted that many times God seems to hide from us. We go through "dark nights of the soul" when we cry out for some sign of God's presence, but he doesn't give us one. These are severe tests of our faith, because we're not asking for wealth or pleasure, but merely an experience of God. Surely he would want us to experience him, if he cared for us at all.

These are the times when God begins to drop tiny hints of his presence and love. An old friend calls just when we need to hear a friendly voice. "It was so weird," the friend says. "I just had a feeling that I should call you." Or we hear a song on the radio that answers the latest question we've been asking. Or we lose our wallet in a big-city restaurant and a good-hearted waiter chases us two blocks to return it. Minor miracles. Maybe you don't see them as miracles at all. But God is hovering just beyond our radar, a stealth lover. He's the mother who dresses as a bag lady to see her son perform. He wants to support us without influencing us too much.

Søren Kierkegaard told a story of a king who loved a poor maiden in his kingdom, but didn't know how to woo her. If he lavished her with royal gifts—jewels, robes, crowns—she might say that she loved him, but he'd never know whether she really loved him or his gifts. So he decided to disguise himself as a beggar and try to win her heart in smaller ways.

And that's the way God often acts with us. Big miracles would practically force us to love him, but when God plays hard to get, our devotion grows deeper.

The Nature of Things

Imagine a conference featuring some of the great novelists and playwrights of our day. Among all the literary lions is one young woman who is sure she doesn't belong. After all, she's sitting next to the author of a novel that insightfully examines the human condition, bringing characters together and pulling them apart in poignant and deeply meaningful ways. On the other side is a playwright whose dialogue is packed with existential questions, probing the needs and doubts of all humanity. As the meeting progresses, the novelist turns to the young woman and asks the question she's been dreading.

"And what do you write, Miss?"

She stammers and stares at her notebook. "Me? Well, nothing much, really. I, uh, I write jokes."

"Jokes?" the novelist repeats, loud enough to make the playwright turn to her, too.

"Well, yes," she replies. "Funny skits for this little comedy group we have in New Jersey."

"And people laugh?" asks the playwright.

"Well, yes," the woman answers cautiously. "They really seem to enjoy themselves." She's embarrassed, ready to run out of the room. She knows she doesn't belong with such giants.

"Jokes," the novelist repeats.

"You make people laugh," the playwright chuckles, giving her a look she can't quite figure out.

She begins her apology: "It's silly, I know, but—"

"Wish I could do that," the novelist announces.

"Me too," says the playwright. "Do you think you could show us how?"

Although God creates masterpieces, he also finds pleasure in the simple things that bring us joy. Sure, God could give every scene of your life a happy ending, but he prefers to sprinkle a few moments of joy throughout your drama.

In *The Problem of Pain*, C. S. Lewis notes that God withholds "settled happiness and security" from us, while he broadly scatters "joy, pleasure, and merriment." He continues, "We are never safe, but we have plenty of fun, and some ecstasy." Why? If we had security in this world, we'd rest in that, and that would keep us from pursuing God. On the other hand, "a few moments of happy love, a landscape, a symphony, a merry meeting with our friends, a bath or a football match, have no such tendency. Our Father refreshes us on the journey with some pleasant inns, but will not encourage us to mistake them for home."[6]

After all, he is the God of the mustard seed and David's slingshot. He won't let Gideon go into battle because his army is too *large,* then sends Gideon up against thousands of enemy troops with an army of 300 armed with kitchen utensils. Repeatedly, "God chose the weak things of the world to shame the strong" (1 Corinthians 1:27). Certainly he could work a stupefying miracle that would overturn the laws of nature to solve all your problems evermore, but that's not his style. He finds delight in wooing us gently.

What Should We Do?

Where are you, God, when I need you? Is that the cry of your heart? Are you angry at God because you feel he has stopped taking your calls? What can you do to ease the pain of apparent abandonment?

Open Your Eyes

Tune in to the tiny miracles around you. God may be hiding around corners, but he's not far from you. Chances are, he's leaving a trail of bread crumbs for you to follow. Kind comments from an unexpected source. A traffic accident averted. The strength you need to get your work done. The gentle whisper within your heart. Stop looking for the fire or earthquake to signal God's presence. Prepare your senses for a quieter message.

Learn to Say "No, But . . ."

One of the cognitive errors many people make is called "Yes, but . . ." No matter what great thing happens to them, they find something wrong: "Yes, I won the lottery, but I'll have to pay a lot in taxes." We're suggesting a reverse method of processing the events in your life. When bad things have happened to you, accept them, but find some silver lining. Look for a bit of good in every tragedy.

We're not talking about denial. The "bit of good" doesn't need to outweigh the disaster in your mind: "Well, I totaled the car, but it's all right because I still have a perfectly good hubcap." That's silly. Face up to the bad stuff, but at least try to find some scrap of goodness.

Show Some Appreciation

Thank God for that "bit of good" in your situation. You may be screaming at him for the tragic circumstances that he allows, but pause a minute and utter a prayer of thanks for that tiny miracle you've discovered. Why? Well, God likes to be thanked. But this may also begin to transform your own attitude. You might begin to see more bits of good in your situation.

Grow for It!

What can you learn from this experience? How can you become a stronger person through this? It's hackneyed now to say that "whatever doesn't kill us makes us stronger," but that's pretty accurate. God is interested in your growth more than in your pleasure or even your physical well-being. He wants your faith to grow. He wants to have a more mature relationship with you.

There's a portion of Isaiah's prophetic writing that addresses the same issues we're addressing—and ends up on a surprisingly upbeat note.

> *Why do you . . . complain, O Israel,*
> *"My way is hidden from the LORD;*
> *my cause is disregarded by my God"?*
> *Do you not know?*
> *Have you not heard?*
> *The LORD is the everlasting God,*
> *the Creator of the ends of the earth.*
> *He will not grow tired or weary,*
> *and his understanding no one can fathom.*
> (Isaiah 40:27-28)

All right, so God is great. We knew that. He has power. But does he care enough to pay attention when we've got problems?

> *He gives strength to the weary*
> *and increases the power of the weak.*
> *Even youths grow tired and weary,*
> *and young men stumble and fall;*
> *but those who hope in the LORD*
> *will renew their strength.*
> *They will soar on wings like eagles;*
> *they will run and not grow weary,*
> *they will walk and not be faint.* (Isaiah 40:29-31)

CHAPTER SIX

"FORGIVING" GOD

"**I** spit on God!" And with that, Helen loudly spat on the floor. At this point in her life, she was in America, married with three children, and living in her own home in Philadelphia, which she kept fastidiously clean. No one else would dare track dirt across her well-scrubbed floor, but she wanted to make a point, so she spat. It was her way of summing up all the anger from her tragic life experience. If God existed, he was her worst enemy.

In the last chapter, we left Helen on the dock in New York, having been rejected by a potential husband and sponsored by a minister. With that sponsorship, she could get off Ellis Island and settle in America. The minister already had a family—he had no desire to support Helen, too—so he kept in touch with the Jamgochian family and especially with Michael Jamgochian, the potential husband.

Yes, Michael was disappointed that Helen was not the beautiful girl he had corresponded with. Yes, she had no right to take the money and come to America in her friend's place. Apparently, he had even learned that Helen had lived "as a wife" of a Turkish officer, and thus she was no longer a virgin—"damaged goods." Yes, all of that was true, the minister would tell him, but surely all of that could be overcome. Here she was, a seventeen-year-old Armenian girl who had been through a horrendous experience, needing a husband, and Michael was an Armenian man needing a wife.

"What else are you going to do—send for another wife and write more letters and send more money and maybe the same thing will happen? Make the best of a bad situation. Marry her."

The minister was persuasive. Over the objections of his parents, three days after her arrival, Michael Jamgochian married Helen. You might consider that the end of Helen's thrilling adventure. Somehow she had survived the death march, virtual slavery, a harrowing escape, frostbite, and the journey to a new land. Case closed. But Helen's spiritual turmoil was far from over.

As she saw it, she had succeeded in making a life for herself, despite all the obstacles God had thrown in her way. She finally had some peace, but she was determined that God would never have a place in her life. She continued to hold a major grudge. God was dead to her.

Her conflict became even clearer several years after her wedding when she finally sent for her mother to come and live with her. Helen had known for some time now that her mother had survived the death march and had settled in Bulgaria. Helen's anger toward her mother for her unrealistic faith and its tragic consequences, as Helen saw it, finally cooled enough for their long-delayed reunion.

Helen and her mother were night and day, spiritually speaking. As bitter as Helen was against God, her mother, Anna, was just as sweetly faithful. While her mother sang hymns of joy, Helen cursed. Anna would pray and praise the God who saw her safely through the desert, and Helen would spit.

I (Michele) have memories from my childhood of my grandmother, Helen, and great-grandmother, Anna, arguing constantly—often about God. Anna, now quite elderly, would get her pension check and ask Helen to give most of it to the church. Helen wouldn't do it. "Why should that bunch of frauds get your good money? I need it more than they do."

Helen's children, including my mother, grew up without religious instruction in the home. As a result, I had very little religious influence in my childhood. As a teenager I became a Christian, and afterward I began to take the place of my great-grandmother in those religious discussions with Helen. The discussions would continue for twenty-seven years.

At first, Helen refused to believe that there was a God. "But Grandmom," I would say, "look at the world around us—the flowers, the grass, the sky. How could that just happen?"

"But Michele, look at the terrible events in the world," the older woman would counter. "How could God let that happen?"

"But, Grandmom, how can you be so angry at someone who doesn't exist?"

Eventually, Helen allowed for God's existence, but added, "He may be real, but he's rotten."

I became a pain to my ministers and professors, badgering

them with tough questions, seeking answers to take back to my grandmother.

"He doesn't keep his promises," Helen would grouse.

"What promises, Grandmom? What has he promised you?"

"He's supposed to make life better."

"Where does he promise that?"

"In the Bible."

"But where? Let's find it. I see that he promises to be with us in our suffering, but he never says life will be easy."

"It's in there somewhere."

As an adult, now a psychology professor, I gained great insight from Philip Yancey's book *Disappointment with God,* which we have cited in this book. For once, someone allowed that it's normal to be disappointed, even angry, with God at times. Why not talk with God about it? I had seen the dangers of suppressing negative feelings, so I began to encourage my grandmother to tell God how angry she was. Of course Helen resisted.

"Just talk to God about it, Grandmom. Let him know how you feel."

It became a personal crusade for me, and all the more urgent as my grandmother was diagnosed with cancer.

"Here's a promise that we know God has made, Grandmom. He promises eternal life for those who trust in him. Why don't you stop blaming him for promises he hasn't made and start claiming a promise he *has* made?"

But I was getting too intense. The harder I tried to persuade my grandmother, the more resistant my grandmother became. Finally I decided to stop worrying and let God take over the job. God could take care of my grandmother.

The next day, when I saw Grandmom, I knew something had changed. "What happened, Grandmom?"

"I did it," Helen answered with a coy smile.

"Did what?"

"I talked to him."

"Who?"

"God," Helen finally spelled out. "Maybe you'd better call that minister fellow of yours. I think it's time for me to forgive God."

Overjoyed, I did call that "minister fellow," the pastor of my church, who came to Helen's bedside with some other church members to counsel her and to serve her Communion. The woman who had suffered so much was finally making peace with the one who suffered for her.

The Problem with "Forgiving" God

You might bristle at the idea of "forgiving" God. Many do. In fact, as we have discussed the theme of this book with friends and colleagues, a number of people track with us easily *up to this point.* "Angry with God? Right. Be honest about your feelings? Absolutely. Express them to God? You said it. Forgive God? Now wait a second!"

The problem stems from our definition of *forgiveness.* In common parlance, it implies that the one being forgiven has done wrong, as in "Forgive us our *trespasses.*" No trespasses, no need for forgiveness. Since God has never done anything wrong, we don't need to forgive him. In fact, some worry that to think of forgiving him might indicate a dangerously low view of God.

But you can relax. We're not saying that God has sinned. We believe he is perfectly righteous in all his acts, even when we don't get what he's doing. And that's the issue: perception. For most of her life, Helen felt that God had wronged her. As we have seen, she had a number of rather persuasive reasons to feel this way—even though our theology dictates that God does no wrong to anyone.

Now Helen had opened up to God about her feelings. She had expressed her anger, imperfect as it was, and now she wanted to make peace with God. She had two paths to choose from:

1. She could adopt a theology that says God is totally perfect and therefore she, as a sinner, either deserved what she got or is completely incapable of understanding the ways of God.

2. She could continue to believe that God wronged her, but let go of her hatred in order to have a friendship with God—that is, "forgive" God.

For too long, religious leaders and institutions have been demanding that people take the first route. But most people who are angry at God, like Helen, aren't ready for that route. God is a stranger to them.

We advocate that hurting people hang out a while with God before they start theologizing. Let's remove the roadblocks to relationship first—and then we can let God reveal to the person more about himself.

If you see forgiveness as a legal statement, then "forgiving" God is a contradiction. God is not guilty, so he needs no pardon. But if you see forgiveness as a relational step, it's a different story.

One of my (Randy's) earliest memories is something I don't remember. I was four, and my neighbor said he saw me picking his flowers. Now, Mr. Smith spent a lot of time gardening, so flower-picking was a major offense. My mom got the phone call and sternly asked me to go next door and apologize. But I insisted that I didn't do it. To this day, I insist that I didn't pick the flowers. I remember playing in the Smiths' front yard with my best friend, Greg. Maybe Greg picked some flowers, but not me.

My mom called Mr. Smith back and asked if maybe Greg was the flower-picker. No, Smith insisted, it was that little scoundrel Randy.

Two things happened next. First, my mom made it clear to me that she believed in my innocence. Second, she asked me to go apologize anyway, because it was important to have a good relationship with Mr. Smith.

I did so. "I'm sorry if I picked your flowers." The *if* was very important. "I won't do it anymore."

As a legal dispute, this could have grown ugly. But the Petersens short-circuited all that by asking for forgiveness and restoring the relationship with their neighbor. Smith was operating with a mistaken perception—as we do in our anger against God. But it would have taken too long to change that perception. Once the relationship was restored, Smith could see what a wonderful little child Randy really was, but in that moment forgiveness was needed to reconnect these people. In the same way, those who feel wronged by God need to offer forgiveness in order to get back on speaking terms with him. Then they can see more of who he really is.

What Is Forgiveness?

When we look at forgiveness solely within the context of restoring relationships, we understand that the key figure is the forgiver, rather than the one being forgiven. It doesn't really matter how big the offense is, whether it's real or imagined, or even if the offender wants to be forgiven—forgiveness can still occur. You can decide all by yourself, while driving or shaving or sleeping, that you forgive an ex-spouse or a dead parent or your health insurance company. Or you can sit with an estranged loved one through a teary reunion, exchanging forgiveness. Forgiveness comes in a variety of forms, but it has the following basic components:

- ≪ I feel wronged by what you've done.
- ≪ I am committed to this relationship.
- ≪ I let go of my bad feelings toward you.
- ≪ Let's wipe the slate clean.
- ≪ Let's start over on new terms.

I Feel Wronged by What You've Done

There are two main pieces here: my feelings and your actions. Note that the "I-statement" can soften the accusation: *I could be wrong, but this is how I feel, and my feelings stem from your behavior. I need to name the offense and the offender.*

Some tend to think of forgiveness as a shrugging off of an offense, or an excusing of it: "How can I forgive him for that? It was *wrong!*" Well, that's the whole point. If it wasn't wrong, why would you need to forgive? Forgiveness is very confrontational, accusing. It has to name the crime before dealing with it.

Try this: go to your place of business and start saying to people, "I forgive you." What kind of reaction will you get? Some will think you're crazy, but others will be offended. "You forgive *me?* Just who do you think you are, forgiving me like that? What have I done to you?"

Why the negative response to such a loving act? Because forgiveness starts with accusation.

But the I-statement gives us some wiggle room, especially when we're "forgiving" God. We must allow for the fact that our perceptions may be skewed. We need to be honest about our feelings, but we should also realize our feelings might be honestly wrong. A number of people feel hurt by the death of their parents or other loved ones. In their skewed perceptions, they're actually mad at the person for dying. They know this makes no sense, but that's the way they feel. Because it's so ridiculous, they often keep themselves from going through the forgiveness process, but that's exactly what they need.

"My father died when I was a small child," reported a student in one of my (Michele's) classes. "I remember being very mad at him for dying."

The same thing happens with God. People know they must be mistaken, because God can do no wrong—but they still feel angry. And they still need to go through the forgiveness process.

That first statement still holds: *I feel wronged by what you have done.* That's the essence of the anger-with-God problem, and we need to bring that honestly to God.

I Am Committed to This Relationship

When there *is* a relationship, this is a key component of the forgiveness process. When a husband and wife need to clear the air, step one can be hard to take without step two. "You have hurt me!" is an attack (even with the proper I-statement). But it takes on a different tone when it's followed by something like: "I only say this because I love you very much and I want us to have a good relationship."

Every day, you feel wronged by people you don't bother to forgive. Someone cuts you off in traffic, jostles you on the subway, or shortchanges you at the market, and you shrug it off *because that relationship doesn't matter to you.* Let jerks be jerks; you won't let it bother you. A minute later, you have forgotten the offense.

But forgiveness becomes important when you care about a relationship. This applies to all sorts of relationships, casual as well as serious. If you shop regularly at the market where you were shortchanged, you have a kind of relationship there, and so you might want to confront the guilty clerk or the manager. You have different kinds of relationships with coworkers, neighbors, and distant relatives. The need for forgiveness varies with your commitment to whatever kind of relationship you have.

This even applies to past relationships. You may need to forgive someone you'll never see again. This happens frequently in divorce recovery. She runs off to Rio and he hates her for two years, but then he decides he must forgive her *unilaterally.* He lets go of the hatred (more on that later) because he still has a relationship with *the memory of her.* He wants to be able to think back on the time he spent with her without dredging up those hateful feelings.

Obviously, with God the relationship can be current or deep in the past. For Helen, it was a distant memory. She had closed God out of her life since she was a little girl, but now she wanted a new relationship with him. The situation might not be so drastic for you. Maybe you've had a fairly good relationship with God, but you've slammed a few doors on him. Now, for the good of the relationship, you're reopening those doors.

I Let Go of My Bad Feelings Toward You

It sounds so simple, doesn't it? Just *let go*. But that's exactly what it is. When people do this, they feel a weight lifted off their shoulders, almost literally, and they wonder why they didn't do it sooner.

"Forgiveness suspends resentment or hostility, liberates the offending party and makes possible a restored relationship," writes one psychologist.[1] Another team of experts says:

> "Forgiveness has been defined as a voluntary forswearing of negative affect and judgment by an injured party directed at someone who has inflicted a significant, deep, and unjust hurt; this process also involves viewing the wrongdoer with love and compassion. In general, this is a process of struggling with and ultimately abandoning negative thoughts, feelings, and behaviors directed at the injurer, while gradually and actively incorporating positive thoughts, feelings, and behaviors toward the same."[2]

Suspending, liberating, forswearing, abandoning—all of that is psychospeak, of course, for the basic act of *letting go* and allowing positive feelings to replace the negative ones.

Our grudges weigh us down, and yet we hang on to them for dear life. Lewis Smedes tells an old European fable about a man named Fouke whose wife, Hilda, had been unfaithful. He said he forgave her, but he held a grudge within: "So each time that Fouke would feel his secret hate toward Hilda, an angel came to him and dropped a small pebble . . . into Fouke's heart. . . . Thus he hated her the more; his hate brought him pain and his pain made him hate."[3]

What an apt description of the weight of hatred in our hearts! Pebbles, dragging us down, and a new one every day. That's what happens when we nurse anger against other people and against God. That's why the Bible tells us, "Do not let the sun go down while you are still angry" (Ephesians 4:26).

In the fable Smedes tells, the pebbles weigh Fouke down until an angel urges him to ask for "magic eyes." Then he would be able to see his wife "as a needy woman who loved him instead of a wicked woman who betrayed him."

Fouke got the magic eyes, and the angel "lifted the pebbles from Fouke's heart, one by one, though it took a long time to take them all away. Fouke gradually felt his heart grow lighter; he began to walk straight again."

Yes, sometimes it takes quite a while to unload the grudge from your heart, but in some cases it happens quite suddenly. No doubt Helen had been mulling this over, but when she finally decided to let go of her anger, the restoration of her relationship with God was very swift.

What is this "letting go"? It's a conscious decision to allow good feelings to replace bad ones. When we hold onto our anger, we develop mental reflexes that bring hatred to our hearts whenever we think of the offending person. By letting go of the bad feelings, we override those reflexes. We say no to the hatred as it begins and we choose to think positive thoughts instead. For some people this requires a great deal of mental and emotional discipline. For others, it's like flipping a switch.

Our friend Lisa has told us about the struggles of growing up with a birth defect that affected her eyesight and hearing and paralyzed one side of her face. Her classmates were brutal, mercilessly teasing and abusing her, but Lisa maintained a forgiving spirit. "I knew that most of those kids weren't trying to be mean," she says. "They were just trying to take negative attention away from themselves." They threw lots of mistreatment at her, but she was like Teflon—nothing stuck. That's what forgiveness does.

On the other hand, Lisa's mother held grudges. She was bitter about Lisa's problems and about being deserted by her husband. Throughout her life, she was angry at people and at God. But Lisa, despite the extent of her own problems, never blamed God. "God must have given me a coping mechanism," she says. That's the "forgiveness switch" we're talking about. Lisa's mom had it turned off, and she held on to every offense. Lisa's forgiveness was humming away in the "on" position.

Smedes' image of the "magic eyes" is helpful. It might just mean a change in how we see the offender, just as Lisa was able to see her tormentors as needy people themselves. When we do that, feelings of compassion can replace the feelings of hate and revenge. And that's why we have already spent so much time on the issue of your God-image. If you see God as Santa Claus, you'll feel cheated. If you see him as an austere judge, you'll feel condemned, with no way to appeal. If you see him as a bumbling inventor whose creation has gotten away from him, you'll feel victimized by his ineptness.

But what if you see him as a powerful Creator who loves his creatures in a deep but complex way? What if you see that he suffers along with you? What if you begin to see the little miracles he does along the way? Then you just might be able to let go of the pebbles that have been weighing you down.

Let's Wipe the Slate Clean

Forgiveness isn't just about feelings; it's also about obligation. In our various interpersonal transactions, we can let go of our hatred for past offenses but still hold the offender liable.

Tammy needed a car. Her older brother, Bob, was about to trade in his car on a newer model, but he let her take his old car instead. It was worth a couple thousand dollars, but Bob knew Tammy was struggling financially, so he was willing to delay payment a year or two until she was better off. Those years passed, and although Tammy began to make more money, she didn't pay for the car. Bob would drop hints occasionally, but Tammy either missed them or ignored them. This became a source of resentment for Bob. He noticed that he treated Tammy badly at family get-togethers—not intentionally, but apparently his subconscious wanted revenge.

Finally, one Thanksgiving, after a particularly strong hint went nowhere, Bob decided to let it go. His love for his sister was worth more than the couple thousand dollars she owed him. "You know that money you owe me for the car?" he mentioned after dinner. "Forget about it. It's a gift."

He "forgave" the debt. It would be one thing to dismiss the ill feelings he had gathered over the years of her nonpayment, but it was quite another to write off the debt. That's what we mean by wiping the slate clean. It's an agreement to act as if the offense didn't happen.

It *did* happen. Both parties know it. But they're agreeing not to let that affect their relationship. Maybe you've been pulled over for a traffic violation and then let go without getting a ticket. The cop gives you a stern warning to drive more carefully, but as far as the government is concerned, you're innocent of wrongdoing.

In one of the many legal dramas on TV these days, an attorney snaps at the judge and the judge glares back, saying, "I'm going to forget you said that." What does that mean? Will the judge undergo hypnosis to remove the offending comment from her brain? Of course not. But the judge was deciding not to let that comment affect the case. Yet she fully expected the lawyer to remember never to do that again.

"Forgive and forget" doesn't entirely work. As Lewis Smedes says, "If you forget, you will not forgive at all. You can never forgive people for things you have forgotten about."[4] Another book on restoring relationships adds, "Forgiveness is *like* forgetting because, as we heal, the painful memories move further and further from our active minds. . . . The hurtful event becomes less important to us. The memory is *there*; it just doesn't keep hurting us anymore."[5]

So "wiping the slate clean" isn't a complete forgetting. It's a decision to act as if it never happened.

It's interesting to note that the Hebrew word used most often in the Old Testament for forgiveness literally means "covering." Theologically, we'd love to find a root meaning of "erasing" or "disintegrating." Doesn't God "do away with" our sin? Well, sure, and the Old Testament does mention God "cleansing" or "removing" our sin, but the major Hebrew concept of forgiveness is that God covers our sin. "Forgiveness is *concealing,* or hiding an offense and thus removing it from consideration," notes one scholar, quoting Psalm 32:1, "Happy are those whose . . . sin is *covered*" (NRSV, emphasis added).[6]

What does this mean, then, when we "wipe the slate clean" with God? We're used to needing him to cover over our sin; how can we do that for him?

First, it means that we decide that he doesn't owe us anything. God himself spoke to Job in legal terms when he said,

> *"Who has a claim against me that I must pay?*
> *Everything under heaven belongs to me."*
> (Job 41:11)

Paul picked up the idea in Romans: "Who has ever given to God, that God should repay him?" (11:35).

Even when we let go of our bad feelings, we still harbor expectations that the Santa-God owes us more than we're getting. We need to clear the books. We can deal with God on his own terms, letting him be the kind of God he wants to be.

Second, "wiping the slate clean" with God means that we stop holding his past deeds against him. This is difficult to talk about, because it seems that we're treating God as a sinner, but let's give it a try. Let's say that you hold God responsible for the terrible bloodshed in Rwanda a few years back. It was tribal warfare at its grisliest, and many of the killers were churchgoing people. How could God let something like that happen?

So let's say that, whenever you've thought about God for the past few years, you've grown angry at the thought of this Rwandan atrocity. But now you're trying to get past that, so you've let go of your bad feelings. Now it's time to stop blaming him for that and wipe the slate clean.

In this step, you give him the benefit of the doubt. You assume he has a good explanation—even though you still don't get it. You decide to move forward with this relationship *as if the offense had never happened.* It did happen; you're not denying it. But you're choosing not to focus on it. You're choosing to cover it over so that you can proceed with a new relationship.

Let's Start Over on New Terms

Sometimes people think that forgiveness just puts things back where they were, like that episode of the TV series *Dallas* where a character woke up and realized the previous season was just a dream. But the truth is, every forgiveness involves a change in a relationship. Both parties need to learn from the events and move forward. You can't go back.

But weren't we just saying that "wiping the slate clean" means pretending the offense never happened? Well, that's the dual nature of forgiveness. You don't really forget, but you don't focus on remembering. You let go, but you learn. You clear the books so that the offender doesn't owe you anything anymore, but you also find new ways of relating to that person.

Let's go back to Bob and his sister Tammy. He eventually forgave her the debt for the car, but what if she asks to borrow money for a down payment on a house? "I'll pay you back, honest!" she says, but Bob knows her track record. He has completely forgiven her for the car episode, but now the relationship exists on new terms. He may establish a formal, notarized loan with a clear payment schedule and penalties for late payment. And he would probably require a lien against the house. Or out of sheer kindness he might *give* her the money she needs, but he wouldn't expect repayment. He has learned that she's not good with debts, and he responds accordingly.

Parents might forgive a teenager for sneaking out after curfew, but you can't blame them for setting stricter rules and watching the teenager like a hawk for a while. The kid has to regain trust. It's not a grudge they're holding; it's common sense they're applying.

Divorced people deal with this sort of thing as they seek to forgive their ex-spouses. They don't expect the damage to be undone. They know they won't wake up from this dream. But they still need to reach a peace about their changed relationship. In the case of unilateral forgiveness—where they'll never see the spouse again—they're seeking peace for their memories. "Starting over on new terms" means they start their own lives over, free from the hatred they've been harboring. But many divorced people need to stay in touch with their former spouses—for the kids, for finances, or for some other reason. Forgiveness is important, but so are those "new terms." They don't want to let themselves be hurt again.

Often forgiveness requires a certain amount of negotiation. First, there could be some discussion about what exactly the offense is. You may be mad at your neighbor for A, B, and C, but your neighbor only admits to A. B isn't half as bad as you think, and you're totally misinterpreting C. Ideally, you can talk this through and reach a better understanding of each other.

But negotiation may also be necessary for these "new terms" of the relationship. After forgiveness, what kind of relationship will you have? What are the rules? How will you protect yourselves and each other? How will you restore trust? This stage of the forgiving process is hard work. You're starting over. It's a whole new ball game, and you probably don't know how to play it perfectly.

What does all this have to do with "forgiving" God?

After you've let go of your bitterness, and after you've released God from the debts you've been holding against him, you are free to start a new relationship with him. As with any human relationship, you can't go back. Some people fear that resolving their God-anger will take them back to their Sunday school days, when they trusted God merely because that's what their parents wanted. But that's not the case at all. Resolution moves you *forward*. You have wrestled with God and now it's time to do something new.

As with a human relationship, negotiation is involved. God may not accept all your charges. He might show you that you need more forgiving than he does. In any case, a whole new kind of relationship awaits.

One idea that will probably change is your image of who God is—and that image may have influenced your anger to begin with. If you've been mad at God as a harsh taskmaster, a negligent Santa, or an absentee father, let him show you who he really is. Build a new life with him, complete with new expectations, new guidelines, and new habits.

Getting Past the Semantics

All of these steps of forgiveness work only if you're willing to take the plunge and "forgive" God. Even people who have turned away completely can resist the notion of forgiving a perfect God. They're uneasy with the idea of setting themselves up as God's forgiving judge—even though the anger in their hearts is judging God for injustice. As Lewis Smedes says, "We plead his case against our own accusations. Your believing mind wants to rush to God's defense against your frightening feelings of hate."[7]

That's why so many people get stuck in their anger. They know they don't want to go back to the blind belief of childhood, but they're afraid to push ahead with the implications of their anger. The way to break this impasse, as we have shown, is to move forward through the anger. If you're angry at God, that means you're feeling he has acted unjustly. Whether he has or not, you *feel* that way. Express your feelings and then offer your forgiveness—even if you suspect that he doesn't need to be forgiven. Save the theology for later; get your feelings out on the table.

Like the four-year-old saying, "I'm sorry if I picked your flowers," you might need to tell God, "I forgive you if you've done anything to be forgiven for." The willingness to forgive puts you on a path of letting go, cleaning the slate, and negotiating a new relationship. Right now you need to be on that path. You can sort out the rights and wrongs farther down the road.

A married couple might go through a period of hurt feelings, harsh words, and distancing. Ideally they come back together after a day or two of that and make up. The conversation might go something like this:

"I'm not sure what I did, but whatever it was, I'm sorry. I can't stand to be enemies like this."

"I know. I'm sorry too."

"Thank you, and I forgive you for any hurt you caused me. Maybe I deserved it."

"Who cares at this point? I'm just glad we're friends again."

We've been using lots of examples from married life, because that's the human relationship that's closest to ours with God.

And this kind of "I forgive you for whatever" is very helpful. Forgiveness is the great equalizer. If you did seven bad things to me and I did four bad things to you, and then we forgive each other, the scoreboard doesn't matter anymore. Forgiveness resets both scores to zero.

If my feelings say God has done five big things wrong to me and my mind says it's impossible for him to do anything wrong, forgiveness brings me to a point of agreement. It wipes the slate clean and allows me to start a new relationship with God on new terms.

Are you reluctant to offer God your forgiveness? That might be because you're still clinging to your false images of who God is supposed to be. Or perhaps you're so invested in your anger that you don't know any other way to live. (We can get trapped in certain emotional patterns that begin to seem normal to us.) Maybe you're afraid to drop the charges because this "new relationship on new terms" scares you silly. You might actually have to deal with a God you haven't created yourself.

Or you might still be denying that you have anything to be mad about. The anger is gnawing away at your soul, but you want to pretend that everything's fine. "Forgiving" God seems blasphemous to you because he's supposed to be the judge, not you. And you're right—but as a result, you've steered clear of his courtroom. You're avoiding him, ignoring the wooing of his Spirit, and that's even worse than blasphemy. As we've defined forgiveness, it's a letting go and a reaching out for a new relationship. That's not arrogant or rebellious; it's an expression of love and peace.

Pierre Wolff puts this beautifully: "When people can express harsh feelings to the One or ones who are their object, love is already stronger in them than their feelings. Love is already transforming, transfiguring, this feeling into something else, something closer to love than to hatred. The power of the Resurrection is *already* working in them. Perhaps there is hatred present as long as people are mute, absolutely mute; but as soon as they decide to express what is in their heart to the other, something is *already* changing and maybe even *already* changed. . . . This expression is a desire for reconciliation."[8]

Don't stay mute and let your anger simmer. Speak out, reach out, and dare to discover a new relationship with the one who made you.

CHAPTER SEVEN

FINDING FORGIVENESS

"Forgiving" God was an important step for Helen, and long overdue. She was unburdened. Releasing her anger had taken a load off her heart. Though she was still bedridden with her illness, she seemed to be sitting up higher than before, no longer sunk down by the weight of bitterness. These events sparked some spiritual restoration in other family members, who were seeing subtle changes in their indomitable matriarch. But a few days later, Helen was troubled again.

"What's the problem, Grandmom?" I (Michele) asked her.

Helen slowly put her thoughts together: "You know last week I forgave God. And it felt good. But now I am wondering if God will forgive me. I've done things I am not proud of in my life. Do you think the minister fellow can come back to talk with me?"

I smiled and patted my grandmother's hand. "I think we can arrange that."

The minister fellow came the next morning.

"It wasn't enough," Helen told him.

"What wasn't?"

"Forgiving God," she said, staring out her window as if reading some billboard out there. "It was good but it wasn't enough."

"Why wasn't it enough, Helen?"

"I've been thinking," she said, and the minister could see that she had been wrestling with these thoughts for several days. "I forgave him for the things he did to me, but then I saw all the things I did to him. I—" and her eyes began to moisten, "I haven't been very good to him."

The minister thought about reassuring her but stayed silent for the moment. She needed to get this out.

"I've done some things in my life that I am not proud of. I have done some terrible things," she continued. "Do you think . . . do you think God could ever forgive me?"

"Yes, Helen," the minister replied with a deep-set smile, "God can forgive you, and he does. That's why Jesus came, to forgive even the worst of sinners. The Bible says that when we confess our sins, God is faithful and just and he will forgive us our sins, and cleanse us from everything we've done wrong."

Helen was having a hard time letting this message get through. "But I've done some things I am not proud of, some terrible things," she repeated, shaking her head.

"I know," the minister replied, "but it's not about our goodness. It's about his. The Bible says we are saved by God's grace, through faith, not through our own works of righteousness. Jesus forgave the thief next to him on the cross, and he will forgive you."

"But—" she began, and trailed off.

The minister allowed the Spirit to work in silence, but then felt moved to add, "Just as you let go of your bitterness against God last week, God is ready to let go of all his bad feelings toward you. He forgives you, Helen. He loves you very much."

She finally got it. As she looked straight at the minister, a smile came to her face. The hardness of eighty years of hatred was melting before his eyes, and she suddenly looked as soft as a newborn baby. Helen then turned toward the window and looked into the heavens. Raising her arms in that direction, she said the most heartfelt "thank you" the minister had ever heard.

After the minister left, Helen was filled with a sense of heavenly peace, as if angels were already in the room with her. After explaining to me that she had finally made up with God, she added, "You know, a lot of people would think that I had it good by making up with God at the end. But it isn't so good. I spent my whole life not knowing that God was there. It's not good to wait so long to make up with God. You tell other people my story, so maybe they won't wait so long."

Those were among the last words I heard my grandmother say. That night, Helen went into a coma, never regaining consciousness. She died a few days later.

Helen held a grudge against God for a lifetime, but she died hoping that you wouldn't do the same thing. As you've seen, she had some pretty serious charges to bring against God, but in the end she let them go in order to grasp his eternal love.

What charges do you bring against your Creator? Have you encountered personal hardship, or do you rail against the human condition in general? In this book we have sought never to minimize your complaints. On the contrary: if people are paying attention at all, there are many things in this world that can and should upset them. It only makes sense to lash out in anger against God.

But anger is like guacamole—an appetizing taste for the moment, but it doesn't keep well. Lash out in anger, if that's what you're feeling, but don't store it up—it will rot within you. *In the moment,* anger alerts you to something that seems wrong to you. You're honing your God-given sense of justice as you storm God's throne to plead your case. But after you have your say, let God have his. Listen to him humbly, and be willing to admit that there might be a few things you don't understand. Let your anger lead you closer to God. Let it open doors rather than slam them. Offer a kind of forgiveness to God in order to claim a new relationship with him, and be wise enough to ask for his forgiveness, too.

Stepping Out of Our Circle

Anger is myopic. In the heat of passion, we see only our own rights, and how we have been wronged. The whole world takes on two dimensions: us and them; right and wrong; good and evil; fairness and unfairness. With those blinders on, we ignore any shades of gray. Mitigating circumstances stop mitigating, and we become blind to our own errors. After all, we're on the side of right, good, and fairness. How could we be wrong?

So you get steamed at the car that's tailgating you and flashing its lights. That's rude, morally repugnant, and illegal. Never mind the fact that you're in the left lane on a highway with signs saying "Keep right except to pass." That traffic law *doesn't matter* when the other guy is flouting the tailgating regulations. We easily puff up the other guy's crimes while excusing our own. We have entered a battle, and it's treason to sympathize with the other side or to criticize our own. We are on the side of right.

Most marriages go through a post-honeymoon stage in which the spouses take sides. Up until that point, everything has been about the relationship—us, us, us. But in this stage of negotiation, each spouse starts establishing his or her own rights—me, me, me. This isn't as dastardly as it sounds—good relationships involve both *us* and *me*—but things turn sour quickly when the two *mes* become enemies. Suddenly each partner begins to tally up the offenses of the other, but they are hardly impartial. Each partner's analysis is seriously skewed in his or her own favor. That's what anger can do.

Marriage counselors try to inject a third dimension into such relationships—a consideration of the relationship itself. If you can get some *us* thinking back into the *me* versus *me* conflict, there's hope for the marriage. Each partner needs to look beyond his or her own needs and complaints in order to see the larger picture. What's best for the relationship?

The same thing is true in our conflict with God. We can go for years—as Helen did—chronicling the supposed misdeeds of our Creator. It's us against him, and every little injustice in the world gets listed on his rap sheet. We feel perfectly justified as we charge him with these crimes. After all, he's the one who has let us down. We're the innocent victims.

But God doesn't want to fight with us. He loves us and wants a good relationship with us in which we communicate our feelings and keep growing closer. Life will be so much better if we put down our weapons.

And when we do finally stop fighting God, an interesting thing happens. Our vision changes. Maybe it's the "magic eyes" of that European fable, but we can suddenly see beyond ourselves. Once we cared only about our own situation, but now we see others. Anger closed our sphere of concern to a tight circle around ourselves, but now we see outside the circle, and for the first time we see ourselves reflected in the eyes of others. That can be sobering, and a bit scary. We suddenly see that we're not as perfect as we thought. We're not innocent victims. Maybe we haven't brought all our troubles on ourselves, but we have certainly contributed to some of our problems, and we have caused pain to others, too. We are at least as guilty as anyone else in this fallen world, and maybe our anger has made us more so.

As we saw in Helen's case, "forgiving" God removed the blinders so that she could see her own need for forgiveness. When we release God from the debt we think he owes us, we begin to realize how much we owe him—and how behind we are in our payments.

Forgiving is always about relationships, and relationships have two sides. When forgiveness clears away barriers on one side of a relationship, it makes it easier to remove the barriers on the other side as well. Forgiveness begets forgiveness. That's the wisdom behind that phrase in the Lord's Prayer: "Forgive us our trespasses *as we forgive those who trespass against us.*" When you forgive, you start a chain reaction. Forgiven people forgive others, and forgiving people are humble enough to seek forgiveness.

I Am Not Worthy!

But then there's another trap that awaits us. Once we let down our defenses, we see how needy we ourselves are. We see the sins we have committed, which previously we overlooked. The shock of seeing the brutal truth about ourselves may make us think we have no chance of being forgiven.

That was Helen's last step on her journey of reconciliation. She had finally doused the fires of her anger against God, but now she saw the ashes of her own life. She was genuinely worried that God would not forgive her, that he *could not* forgive her, that she had been his enemy for far too long.

When you spend a lifetime keeping score, it's hard to stop—even when the lead changes hands. Our friend James has an elderly neighbor who often asks him favors, but pays for them with food. If she asks him to pick up some orange juice at the store or fix the color on her TV set, within hours she'll be at his door with a casserole dish. Nothing wrong with this, is there? She just wants to give something back. But once James heard her complaining about another woman who didn't return a favor, and now that woman was her bitter enemy. Obviously James's neighbor was keeping score. He would have been glad to do her favors free of charge, but she thought she was earning those favors with her chicken stew. If James stopped doing those favors, she might get upset. "After all I've done for you," she might say, "you can't go to the corner store for me?"

Many people keep score with God, too. He keeps them healthy—one point for him. They go to church—one point for them. He keeps a speeding truck from running them over—two points for him. They go to church *and* Sunday school—two points for them. He gets them an unexpected tax refund—three points for him. They give a tenth of it to charity—three points for them.

But when God allows something bad to happen, he loses points. They look at the scoreboard, see the imbalance, and say, "After all I've done for you, you can't answer this little prayer for me?" They feel they're justified in their anger because God isn't doing his fair share.

Let's say James and his neighbor have an argument. The neighbor yells at him because he won't go to the corner store, and he proceeds to list everything he's ever done for her: "I've fixed your toaster, moved your furniture, picked up your mail, mowed your lawn, shoveled your snow, cleaned your car, driven you to the hospital, and gone to the store for you 736 times! In exchange, I get chicken stew, which I hate; leftover pot roast, which I can't eat; and stuffed peppers, which make me physically ill."

That would be a major jolt to the neighbor, wouldn't it? She would have to change the score on her scoreboard. Instead of being tied, she's losing 736 to 0! How could she ever make that up? She'd have to cook up filet mignon for him every day for twenty years to get back in the game. As a result, she might be embarrassed, and she might start avoiding him.

Many people who keep score with God are making serious accounting errors. They think they're doing their fair share for him, but when they take the blinders off and stop trying to justify themselves, they see that he is outscoring them by far. This can be depressing to them. How can they outgive God? How can they ever make up the difference? How could he ever forgive them?

They simply have to smash the scoreboard.

Grace Over Fire

You see, God doesn't keep score. Why would he? He wins. In fact, he's in a whole different league. If you're trying to be as good to God as he is to you, forget it. You'll never make it. If you're depressed because you see that you'll never be good enough to win God's forgiveness . . . perk up, because you're playing the wrong game.

"Do you think God could ever forgive me?" That was Helen's heartfelt question the last day of her conscious life on earth. What was she afraid of? She feared that her sins had put her out of God's reach. Her anger, her cursing, her refusal to raise her children in faith—all of this deducted points from her scoreboard. She knew she wasn't good enough for God, so how could he welcome her into his presence? She had stopped fighting him far too late in life, and she hadn't had a chance to do anything good to win his forgiveness.

But what is forgiveness? In the last chapter we discussed its five components. The first was "I feel wronged by what you've done." If there is no feeling of injury, there's nothing to forgive. When we're trying to "forgive" God, our feelings of being "wronged" by him are certainly skewed by our own limited perspective. But when God tells *us*, "I feel wronged by what you've done," we can be sure his feelings are completely valid—we *have* wronged him. But the following steps of forgiveness—including the letting go of bad feelings and wiping the slate clean—have nothing to do with being "good enough." God forgives sin *because it's sin.* If Helen was good enough to earn God's forgiveness, what would he have to forgive?

Ironically then, the crucial question is not "Are you good enough to earn God's forgiveness?" but "Are you bad enough to need it?" Millions of people go blithely through life never asking for God's forgiveness because they think they're doing just fine without it. Helen got to a moment of truth where she realized her spiritual need and begged for God to grant her something she knew she didn't deserve.

The biblical word for this is *grace.* This is not the elegance of a figure skater or the unflappability of a smooth politician. This is the quality underlying God's interaction with human beings. It has to do with giving. When God grants what we don't deserve, that's grace. Grace is the opposite of earning. When you give a friend a gift on her birthday, that's nice but expected. It's sort of a payment for a friendship. She'll reciprocate with a gift on your birthday, so you're even. But when you give this friend a gift just because you were thinking of her and wanted to do something nice, that's grace. And grace is the way God operates.

So when we come to God for forgiveness, we need to realize we're in a whole new ballpark, the stadium of grace. This ballpark has no scoreboard. We need to play by entirely different rules.

God Wants a Relationship with Us

The first idea we need to understand in this regard is that God wants a relationship with us. You can gloss over that as a basic religious truth, but when you think about it, it's astonishing. The Creator of humanity loves you and me individually. We've already seen much of the passion revealed in Scripture—God is crazy about people. He plays the head-over-heels lover even when we stray from him. He created us to enjoy a relationship with him, but he gives us a chance to choose, and he woos us like mad. He's like the adoring adolescent who writes her boyfriend's name all over her notebooks and even on her hands. Consider these words from Isaiah 49:15-16:

> *"Can a mother forget the baby at her breast*
> *and have no compassion*
> *on the child she has borne?*
> *Though she may forget,*
> *I will not forget you!*
> *See, I have engraved you*
> *on the palms of my hands."*

But how can God have a relationship with us when we have been at odds with him? Again and again we have disappointed him, doing the very things he hates. Even when we come to him seeking a relationship, we still do things that offend him. Helen's not the only one who ever felt ashamed about her behavior before a holy God. There's no way we can ever be good enough for him. So if God is going to have a relationship with us, he's going to have to do something radical. He's going to have to forgive us.

And that puts us into the stadium of grace.

We Can't Earn Forgiveness

The next truth we need to accept, as we've already mentioned, is that we can't earn forgiveness. At least not in the way we'd expect. God doesn't forgive you because you're good enough to be worth his while. The only requirement for forgiveness is that you admit that you've done things you need to be forgiven for. And we all have.

Here's what gets some pretty good people in trouble. They haven't committed any major sins, such as murder, adultery, or theft. And they've kept their lying and coveting to a minimum. So they figure they can make up for the minor infractions with some good deeds. They go to church or synagogue, give to charity, visit a nursing home, and say their prayers daily. Surely God will forgive these little sins when he sees how good they are! If they were murderers, they would throw themselves on God's mercy, but they figure they're good enough on their own merits.

What these people are really saying is that they don't need forgiveness because they haven't done anything that bad. They'll pay their own way, thank you very much. Their good deeds will outweigh the bad and God will throw open the doors of heaven to them after he examines their résumé. But that's scoreboard stuff—those people are tallying up their points. And when you start playing that game with God, you lose.

Jesus shocked his generation by announcing that prostitutes and thieves were closer to God's kingdom than religious leaders. Why? Because they knew how desperately they needed forgiveness. They threw themselves on God's mercy, while the self-righteous Pharisees thought they were good enough for God on their own.

Another problem occurs when "bad people" buy what those "good people" are saying. This was Helen's problem. She knew she had been a rebel and her sins were too great to pay for. But she had seen plenty of good people through the years trying to pay for their sins on their own, and she assumed that they were succeeding. Compared to them, she knew she had no chance. That's why she worried that God wouldn't forgive her, because she had committed too many sins to earn his forgiveness. What she didn't realize was that she had something vitally necessary for forgiveness—an awareness of her sin.

That was Jesus' criticism of the Pharisees, too: "Woe to you, teachers of the law and Pharisees, you hypocrites! You shut the kingdom of heaven in men's faces. You yourselves do not enter, nor will you let those enter who are trying to" (Matthew 23:13-14). They taught their "scoreboard mentality" to the common people, who then assumed that they could never be good enough for God—certainly not as good as those religious leaders. But Jesus stunned his disciples by saying their righteousness had to exceed that of the Pharisees. How was that possible? Only if they admitted their sin and accepted God's forgiveness. After healing a blind man, Jesus used this imagery to challenge the self-righteous Pharisees: "If you were blind, you would not be guilty of sin; but now that you claim you can see, your guilt remains" (John 9:41).

Paul took Jesus' message of grace and developed it: "Where sin increased, grace increased all the more," he wrote (Romans 5:20). Yes, that idea is subject to abuse, as Paul anticipated. We mustn't try to sin more so God can forgive us more. But the main point is that we don't have to shy away from God if our sins are great. His grace is always greater.

God's Grace Doesn't Always Seem Fair

A third idea to remember in the stadium of grace is this: God's grace doesn't always seem fair. If you're stuck in a scoreboard mentality, this can make you mad. Anyone would think that a Pharisee would be closer to God than a prostitute; that only makes sense. But God's grace turns things topsy-turvy. Forgiveness is your ticket, not good deeds.

The "minister fellow" who ministered to Helen before her death, Reverend Sturgis Poorman, spoke on this subject in church shortly after her death. His text was a parable told by Jesus, found in Matthew 20:1-16. In this story, a landowner hires day-laborers to harvest his crops. He goes to the marketplace early in the morning and employs a handful of men seeking work. "Come work for me today in my vineyard," he says, "and I'll pay you a denarius." That was the going rate for a full day of harvesting grapes. But as the day went on, he needed more workers, so he went back at 9 A.M., and again at noon, and then 3 P.M., each time hiring another group. "I'll pay you whatever is right," he said. They trusted him to compensate them properly for the amount of work they did.

Finally the landowner returned to the marketplace at 5 P.M., with just an hour left in the working day, to hire a final crew of harvesters. Once again he promised to pay them "whatever is right."

The sun went down and the workers lined up for their pay. The landowner started with those who had worked only one hour, and he gave them each a denarius—a full day's pay! Those who had worked three, six, and nine hours, he compensated in the same way: one denarius. Finally, those who had worked the whole day got their pay—one denarius. Of course, as they saw the money being dished out to those who had worked less, they expected to be paid more. They complained, "Why did you pay us the same amount as you paid the ones who had worked only an hour? That's not fair."

"What was our agreement?" the master responded. "I promised you a denarius for a full day's work, and that's what you got. Are you upset with me because I chose to be kind to others? Don't I have the right to do what I want with my own money?"

There are numerous applications of the basic truth presented in this story. Reverend Poorman referred to Helen as someone who had entered the vineyard late. Because of the grudge she held against God, she stayed out of his kingdom until the last possible hour. Is it fair for her to be welcomed into heaven in the same way as some other dear saint who's been following God for eighty years? Well, no, it's not fair, but it's the way God does things—God's kind of justice. God promises one person, "Follow me all your days and I'll give you eternal life." That person follows him, and he honors his word. He says to Helen, "Trust me in the few hours you have left and I'll do whatever is right," and he grants her eternal life, too. That wreaks havoc on the scoreboard, but it's the way of grace.

In his own context, Jesus was almost certainly referring to the Pharisees and other religious leaders as those who were offended by God's payment plan. They were scorekeepers, and they worked very hard to be more righteous than the common people. They thought they had God's way of justice all figured out. When Jesus came along offering God's grace to prostitutes and the thieving tax collectors, it didn't seem fair. But God has a right to show kindness to anyone, regardless of his or her merit.

The Pharisees were trying to lock God into a system of rewards and penalties for specific actions—a system they could figure out and manipulate to their advantage. Like the all-day workers, they were trusting in the contract. The landowner had agreed: one denarius for one day. But note that the other workers had no contract. They trusted in the master to pay them "whatever was right." Jesus asserted that God would do right, but that he wouldn't always be bound by a contract.

Even today, we can divide religious people into two groups: those who want to "sign a contract" with God and those who trust in his grace. The "contract" people assume that God owes them good treatment if they live good lives. But the Bible makes it clear that no one is good enough for God's holy standards. We all depend on his grace.

The parable of the workers in the vineyard can also help us when we're tempted to go back and reclaim some of our anger. Remember that anger is based on our sense of justice. We get angry when things don't seem fair. But this parable reveals that God's idea of justice is different from ours. We want a detailed system of prorating whereby each laborer gets an appropriate payment per hour worked and per grape picked, minus trans-portation costs and union dues. But God throws that whole sys-tem out. If we're counting on our sense of justice, we're all doomed. All our righteousness amounts to a pile of filthy rags, as the prophet Isaiah said (64:6). Fortunately for us, God's jus-tice is defined by his grace—which means he will do things that don't always make sense to us.

When pain enters our lives, we cry, "What did I do to deserve this?" Well, fundamentally, the answer is that we did a lot to deserve this. Every sin we've ever committed combines to con-demn us to a life of misery and an afterlife of more misery. If we want a fair contract, there it is. Be perfect and live well; be imper-fect and suffer. If the world operated according to our sense of justice, we'd be doomed. Thank God for grace.

As the psalmist sings,

> *He does not treat us as our sins deserve*
> *or repay us according to our iniquities.* (Psalm 103:10)

God's Grace Keeps Giving

The final idea we want you to remember in this stadium of grace is that God's grace keeps giving . . . and giving . . . and giving. After the initial flush of excitement over being forgiven by God, some people begin to worry: "What if I do something wrong now, after God has already forgiven me? Won't that undo the forgive-ness in some way?"

No. Quit toting that scoreboard around with you all the time. God doesn't use it. When you have finally ditched your anger and come to peace with God through forgiveness, you are in a rela-tionship with him. A *relationship*, not a competition. What would a parent say if a child came running up and asked, "How good am I being this week? Am I better than last week? Am I better than my brothers and sisters? How good do I need to be next week? Huh? Huh?" The parent would tell the child to stop worrying. A good relationship includes a desire to please, but not constant scorekeeping.

In our relationship with God, we want to please him. As we grow closer to him, we learn more and more about how to please him. And every so often we fail. We ask him to forgive us again, and he does, welcoming us back into that happy relationship. Does that mean we can get away with a lot of sinful stuff and he'll still forgive us? Well, yes, but that's missing the point. A genuine desire for forgiveness involves a commitment to the relationship, and that means we will want to please God. If you're trying to figure out how many sins you can get away with, you're back to a scoreboard mentality, which you're trying to manipulate.

Peter once asked Jesus, "How many times should I forgive someone who sins against me? Seven times?" Talk about scoreboards! Peter had it all figured out: seven-zip and you call it a shutout. But Jesus said not seven, but "seventy times seven" (Matthew 18:21-22, NASB). No, he wasn't taking the scoreboard up to 490; he was demolishing the scoreboard. Seven was the Hebrew number of completion, perfection. Throw all those sevens together, and he's talking about infinity. Now if Peter is told to keep forgiving forever, how long do you think God will keep forgiving us?

So don't be dismayed when you make mistakes. And don't go back to your habits of defensiveness and self-justification. Get back in the relationship and ask for forgiveness again. As Paul wrote, "I am convinced that neither death nor life, neither angels nor demons, neither the present nor the future, nor any powers, neither height nor depth, nor anything else in all creation, will be able to separate us from the love of God that is in Christ Jesus our Lord" (Romans 8:38-39).

Everyone's situation is unique. Your anger may have different symptoms and different causes from that of anyone else, and so your solutions will have different details. We have discussed various facets of the problem throughout this book, suggesting certain redemptive courses of action. We hope you will adapt the strategies we have offered to fit your particular situation.

Realize that you are where you are in the healing journey. It doesn't help to pretend you're somewhere else. Don't be afraid of your feelings and thoughts. Don't be afraid to give voice to your feelings. Bring them to God for hope and healing.

Appendix

A Diagnostic Guide

In this appendix, we want to summarize our basic points in a way that is useful for review and teaching purposes. We'll consider the following questions:

- ◅ How do you know when you're angry at God?
- ◅ Why do people get angry at God?
- ◅ What can people do about their anger?

How Do You Know When You're Angry at God?

Of course, some people just know. They wear their wrath on their sleeves, and can't stop thinking about how God has let them down.

But many people aren't so obvious about it. Perhaps they haven't totally rejected faith in God, and that's what makes it such a confusing issue for them.

Also, many devout people won't let themselves express their anger at God. They won't even admit that anger is what they're feeling. They hit that wall and they're mystified by it—like some force field on *Star Trek. Why can't I get any closer to God?* In some cases they redirect their anger toward other people, toward the institutional church, or toward themselves. Many people load guilt upon themselves for their "lack of spirituality" when they have psychologically valid reasons for being angry at God. These people often sabotage their own relationship with God because somewhere, down deep, they feel wounded by him—but they may not even realize that's the problem.

In this collection of angry people, where do you fit? Are you overtly angry, or do you hide it, perhaps even from yourself? How many times have these thoughts occurred to you?

- "It isn't fair that God allows bad things to happen to me."
- "I feel that God is so distant from me."
- "I'm afraid to ask God for what I really want."
- "God lets me suffer and doesn't come to help me."
- "It seems as if God is waiting around the corner to trip me up. He's out to get me!"
- "It seems that God is never satisfied with my efforts to please him."
- "I feel so bad about myself. God can't see any value in me."
- "God must be mad at me. He seems to enjoy punishing me."
- "I don't want to pray to God anymore because he doesn't answer my prayers anyway."
- "God doesn't seem to care about me and my problems."[1]

Even when you don't think you're angry at God, or you don't allow yourself to think it, anger might be brewing under the surface. That might explain some of your feelings of victimization or futility or distance from God. Only when you unmask this anger can you defeat it.

Why Do People Get Angry at God?

You might know exactly why you're angry at God, with a detailed description of what he has done to you—and what he *hasn't* done for you. But if you're just coming to terms with your anger, you might have to dig for its source.

Personal Misfortune

Probably the leading cause of anger at God is personal misfortune, such as an accident, an illness, or a disability; perhaps the loss of a job, house, loved one, or marriage. Some people seem to bounce back from such trials with an even stronger faith, but many get rocked by them. This was Helen's situation, of course. The series of personal tragedies she faced overwhelmed her childhood faith, and she turned against God with a vengeance.

The Pain of a Loved One

Some people rail at God not because of their own suffering but because of the pain of a loved one. This anger can be fueled by a strong sense of personal righteousness: "God, apparently I'm a better friend than you are. I'm there for her; where are you?" Often these people get more upset than the ones who are actually suffering, and that can add more fuel to the fire. ("*Someone* has to stick up for you.") While the sufferer can only complain from a standpoint of self-interest, the angry friend is acting in love.

General Injustice of the World

One step removed from that is the person who feels angry because of the general injustice in the world. This might be sparked by a specific painful event such as a shooting in a school, an earthquake, a bombing. But soon it becomes a philosophical battle: "How could God allow these things to happen?"

Bad Representatives of God

Another major reason for anger at God is one we haven't touched on yet: bad representatives of God. For many, these can be their parents. Or perhaps they are church leaders from their childhood. Or even TV preachers. The idea is this—if those are the people who speak for God, and they have treated me badly in his name, God must be as bad as they are. "Psychologically, anger at God can be explained as unresolved anger from previous hurtful relationships which is projected onto God," says William Gaultiere. "People commonly transfer onto God the characteristics of parents and significant others because a relationship with an invisible God is by faith and is developmentally preceded by relationships with parents and significant others."[2] In other words, we grow up assuming that the God we can't see is just like the people who teach us about him. If we get angry at those people, we can easily transfer that anger or disappointment to God, since they appear to be on the same team.

The solution seems simple: in your mind, separate God from those bad representatives. But when everything you know about God has come from those people, that's a tough thing to do. First, there's a logical hurdle. Those are the people in your life who were most committed to God, and if they turned out to be hateful, cruel, or hypocritical, that doesn't say much for God's transforming power. But even if you can understand mentally that God is just as offended by that behavior as you are, there's still an emotional connection you'll find hard to sever. Reverend Brimstone will always seem a bit like God to you because of all those Sundays he thundered down at you from the pulpit. What's worse, God will always seem a bit like Reverend Brimstone. It will take mental and emotional discipline, and perhaps the nurture of a new community of faith, to make the necessary distinctions.

Burnout

Some devout believers develop an underlying anger at God because of burnout. They may be leaders in their churches or charitable causes. They may spend huge chunks of their lives meeting the needs of those around them. They may willingly accept low salaries, or none at all, in order to do the work of the Lord. They tirelessly give themselves to others until there's nothing left to give. *Tireless* may not be the right word, because they *do* get tired, physically and emotionally. And what do they get for all this effort? Not enough. They sense the injustice of unpaid labor, and they seldom complain, but they harbor these feelings against God.

So when they "burn out"—have a nervous breakdown, yell at everyone within earshot, or just walk off the job—they might also ditch their faith. The minister who runs off with the church secretary and its savings account could be motivated by anger as much as by greed and lust, thinking, "I've been a faithful servant for years; now it's my turn to enjoy myself." Since God doesn't seem to be rewarding him enough, he decides to reward himself.

The key to burnout is anticipating it. If you're working too hard and storing up anger, stop. God loves cheerful givers, but he doesn't need overworked, underpaid drudges. Slow down, take a deep breath, and then start to see all the little ways in which God *does* reward you—primarily with the relationship you have with him.

Post-burnout, you probably have a lot of issues to deal with, but first and foremost you must divide God from the work. Stop seeing him as a harsh taskmaster and start letting him lift your burdens. Come to him as a child and let him delight your soul again.

Unanswered Prayer

Another cause of anger against God—one experienced largely by believers—is unanswered prayer. We are taught that prayer works. Some Bible verses seem to give us a blank check: "Ask whatever you will . . ." So when our favorite Aunt Mary gets sick, we pray for her. We beat down the doors of heaven, and we believe with every fiber of our being that God *will* heal her. We name it and claim it and thank God for the answer before it happens, because we know it *will* happen. But it doesn't. Aunt Mary dies, leaving us with a heart full of sorrow and a head full of questions.

You can reinterpret those Bible texts to get God off the hook. You can say that God's "answers" to our prayers include "No" and "Later." Those mental answers may eventually sink in, but our pain is emotional. We still feel that God owed us an answer to our prayer request and he didn't come through. He's not the kind of God we thought he was.

What Can People Do About Their Anger?

Suffering changes our lives. No doubt about it. Although it might be hard to believe right now, those changes may actually improve us. As Freda Crews, host of *A Time For Hope*, often states at her speaking engagements, "Suffering either makes us bitter or better."

Many people mistakenly assume that the only right way to deal with suffering is to demonstrate complete faith, courage, and trust in God throughout the entire process. That's great if you're up to it but what about those who are not? Fortunately for the many who can't do suffering "right," there are other paths to healing. The paths are longer and require more struggling, but they can still end up in the same place as the person who was able to take the shortcut. You might find yourself right now in a maze of suffering, questioning, and anger. Don't despair; there are several paths out of that maze.

Four Tracks

The diagram below shows four common ways of dealing with suffering. The flowchart format indicates the various decisions that a person makes emotionally, intellectually, or spiritually. Along this journey are many forks in the road.

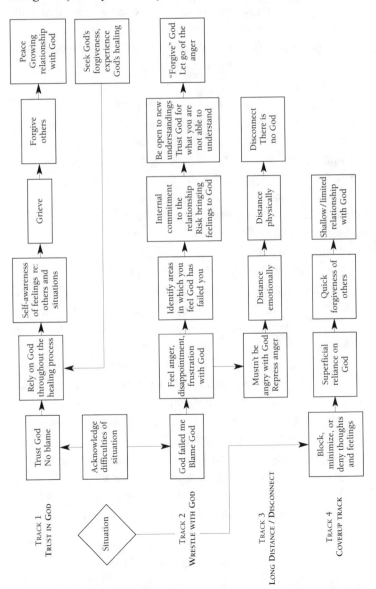

The tracks are not stagnant, nor are they mutually exclusive. At times you will find yourself moving along one track for a life situation and along another track for a different situation. For example, you may be following a "Trust in God" track and trusting God with your love life, while getting involved in a "coverup" of your anger over your mother's illness. At times you may jump tracks. But this model will help you trace a progression of responses in various situations, helping you identify your patterns in relating with God. The model will also help provide a path for healing by showing you the next step or an alternate path to follow.

Track 1: Trust in God

Some people seem to move through life's trials with remarkable faith. While not denying their tragedies or minimizing their struggles, they move forward holding onto God's promises. My (Michele's) great-grandmother, Anna Panosian, survived the Armenian Genocide, a death march, and the loss of three of her children and her husband—and she kept trusting in God the whole time. Until her death, she prayed fervently and worshiped God with all her heart.

The story of Meg Woodson in *Turn It Into Glory* (1991), recounting how she dealt with the death of her child, is a remarkable testament of faith and trust in God during a time of intense personal suffering. So too is Nicholas Wolterstorff's memoir on the loss of his boy, *Lament for a Son* (1987).

Some of our colleagues have recently met with people from Rwanda who have been putting together the pieces of their lives after a season of brutal killings in 1998. They expected to find examples of anger toward God for these horrific events, but instead they found only acceptance. These believers did not expect God to shield them *from* adversity but rather to be with them *in* their adversity. They are focused not on this world, but the next.

Our friend Lisa grew up with the teasing of classmates about a congenital problem that affected her eyes and ears, but she never got onto an angry track. "God puts you through hard things so you can help other people get through them," she says. "You have the option of getting bitter or reaching out to others." And she does reach out in many ways, offering the comfort of her sweet faith to others in need.

On our chart, the "Trust in God" track leads people easily from trial to trust. This does not mean that their lives are easy, but that they somehow are able to respond with faith to their difficulties. When adversity strikes, they cry out, "I'm hurting, God! Please help me through this situation." As a result, they rely on God throughout the healing process, grieving fully and forgiving others as they move forward into a growing relationship with God.

Track 2: Coverup

For many people it's not that simple. The harsh situations of their lives make them angry at God. We don't want to say that the "trust in God" people are better than the others. They just happen to have that coping mechanism that allows them to trust God through the tough times when others respond with disappointment, angry feelings, and hard questions.

But some people try to be "trust in God" people when they're not. They're convinced that's the only legitimate track, so they pretend to trust God when they're really nursing feelings of anger or disappointment. Often they hide their true feelings, even from themselves.

They don't display their anger at God because they have not yet considered that option. They put a box around their thoughts and feelings so they can go through the motions and survive. They don't ask themselves the tough questions because they're afraid of discovering the answers.

On the surface, these folks can often look like the "trust in God" folks. They seem to be moving through the same process, but they are missing the depth of the feelings. They have not yet processed their thoughts. Like an ostrich putting its head in the sand to avoid seeing danger, they often shield themselves from what's really going on within them.

Sometimes these "coverup" people will even quote the Bible as a way to assure themselves and others of their faith. Comforting words from the Bible can be a quick fix, allowing them to deny the real problems they face. Maybe they're not totally denying their problems, but they're minimizing them: "Yes, I've gone through tough times, but God has brought me through." That's a wonderful testimony if the person has actually come *through* his or her trials, but often it's just a way of downplaying the difficulty. Sometimes these people rush to "forgive" God or others before they even realize just what it is that they need to forgive. They'll offer a handshake but hold a grudge.

This is a dangerous track. In their effort to be like the "trust in God" people, these sufferers are denying their suffering. As a result, they never heal properly. All sorts of inner wounds can fester. These people often hit a wall in their relationship with God, unable to grow any deeper and not knowing why. If they dig deeper, they'll find the pain they've buried.

The road to healing for these folks goes backward. They have to *uncover* the feelings they've been denying. For a time, it might seem that they're not very good anymore. They won't look anything like the "trust in God" people they admire. In fact, some observers might think that they've "lost the faith." But in reality they're finding true faith and giving up the charade they've been playing for so long.

Track 3: Wrestle with God

Some find their faith tested when adversity hits. *There is nothing wrong with this.* If you get nothing else from this book, please grab that one idea. It is not a sin to ask God questions. It is not wrong to be honest about your God-given feelings. As we have said, there's an impressive roster of faithful people who have expressed anger, frustration, and disappointment with God. If Moses can do it, you can do it. If *Jesus* can do it, you can do it. The alternative is to bottle up those feelings, stay on Track 2, and live a double life, or to move to Track 4 and distance yourself from God.

Have the courage to be honest with both yourself and God. Denying your feelings won't get you back on track with God, but moving through your feelings will. Dig up those buried grudges and spread them out in the sunshine of God's gaze. Sort through the events that have hurt you. Ask the tough questions.

As you present your case against God, don't edit yourself. You can figure out the validity of your concerns later, but right now just bring your honest feelings and thoughts to the table. Also bring an open heart and an open mind.

If you feel anger, let it out. Express it in a safe environment. Throw some dishes. Or find some understanding friends to complain to. (But don't throw the dishes *at* the friends.) Use your anger for healing. If you're going to duke it out with God, just make sure you're fighting fairly. Throw a few jabs—he can take it. But then don't rush back to your corner; let God answer back.

Bring your grievances to God *for the purpose of reconciliation.* Allow for the possibility that he might have some answers for you, or that he might turn out to be reliable in spite of your frustrations with him. You can "let him have it," but then somewhere down the line you might let him have *you.*

Your dialogue might go something like this: "I'm mad at you, God. I feel you should have done _____. But, because you are important to me, I will at least try to work this out. Even though it may be difficult for me, I am willing to risk bringing my feelings and thoughts to you. And I will be open to understanding it from your perspective."

Once you have tackled your conflicts with God and are able now to feel God's support, you are ready to look at your thoughts and feelings regarding others. Or perhaps you did this step first, saving God for last. Again, emotional healing is not a linear process. Find a way that works for you to move through the process.

The chart outlines the steps we've been presenting in previous chapters. Let your feelings of anger bring you *back* to God, rather than driving you away. Moving *through* the anger, frustration, or disappointment is the way to get back on a track of faith. You will be a stronger person for the process.

Track 4: Long Distance / Disconnect

Some find their faith shattered when adversity hits. They're like the weed-ridden soil in a story that Jesus told. The "seed" of God's truth is planted there and blossoms at first, but soon it is choked by the "weeds." Some of these people might have a limited or untested faith to begin with—like the man in another story who built his house on sand and lost it when the hurricane hit.

Even some who have strong faith face difficulty when the hurricane is stronger. Who can blame the victims of the Armenian Genocide or the Jewish Holocaust or even the Rwandan atrocities for questioning their faith in God? Such tragedies could give anyone second thoughts.

The problem occurs when people shut the door of their heart. Track 4 starts in the same path as Track 3. These people are being honest about their gripes and letting their feelings out. So far, so good. But then there's a fork in the road. Track 3 people turn *toward* God and wrestle with him. Track 4 people let their anger drive them away. Over the next months and years they find themselves distancing themselves from God. Eventually they may disconnect from him entirely, wanting nothing to do with the God they once trusted.

The dialogue may go something like this: "I'm mad at you God. I feel you should have done _____. Oh no, I don't want to be mad at God. It's way too hard to be mad at God. It's disrespectful. It's not allowed. Okay, so I'll just not talk to God for a while until this passes."

Granted, it's not easy to wrestle with God. Many people learn to avoid conflict with other people, and so they have few tools to work through conflict with God. It's easier for them to walk away. And so, rather than listening for any responses God might have to their charges, they drop their bombs and run. They *could* deepen their relationship with God through a heated dialogue, but instead they reject that relationship. They wallow in their pain. In some cases they're trying to get back at God by turning away from him. But in any case, they put distance between themselves and God.

Often it starts with emotional distancing. Such people might continue to go through the motions, attending services and even doing religious work, but their heart isn't in it. They stop praying, except by rote, and they no longer sense God's guidance in the Bible. The next step is physical distancing, usually a rejection of one's religious affiliations. A person stops going to church or quits a charitable commitment. Ultimately there might be the final disconnection of denying God's existence (this can take the form of *functional atheism,* in which a person gives mental assent to God but acts as if he doesn't exist).

Once again, the road to healing goes backward. Retrace the steps away from God and get back to the point of expressing anger *to* God. That gets you back on Track 3 and the renewed possibility of a thriving relationship with God.

REFERENCES

Allender, Dan, and Tremper Longman. *The Cry of the Soul.* Colorado Springs, CO: NavPress, 1994.

Belz, J. "Anger: A Little Like Sex: A Few Guidelines for Keeping a Noble Instinct on Track." *World,* 15 October 1994, p. 3.

Blocher, Henri. *Evil and the Cross.* Downers Grove, IL: InterVarsity, 1994.

Bonar, Clyde A. "Personality Theories and Asking Forgiveness." *Journal of Psychology and Christianity* 8 (1): pp. 45-51 (1989).

Carney, Sheila. "God Damn God: A Reflection on Expressing Anger in Prayer." *Biblical Theology Bulletin* 13: pp. 116-120 (1983).

Cerling, Charles E., Jr. "Anger: Musings of a Theologian/ Psychologist." *Journal of Psychology and Theology* 2: pp. 12-17 (1974).

Cerling, Charles E., Jr. "Some Thoughts on a Biblical View of Anger: A Response." *Journal of Psychology and Theology* 2 (4): pp. 266-268 (1974).

Childs, Brian H., and David W. Waanders (editors). *The Treasure of Earthen Vessels: Explorations in Theological Anthropology.* Louisville, KY: Westminster John Knox Press, 1994.

Christ, Carol P. "Expressing Anger at God." *Anima* 5 (1): pp. 3-10 (1978).

Claypool, John. *Tracks of a Fellow Struggler: Living and Growing Through Grief.* New Orleans: Insight Press, 1995.

Compaan, Arlo. "Anger, Denial and the Healing of Memories." *Journal of Psychology and Christianity* 4 (2): pp. 83-85 (1985).

Cunningham, Bobby B. "The Will to Forgive: A Pastoral Theological View of Forgiving." *The Journal of Pastoral Care* 39 (2): pp. 141-149 (1985).

Davis, Stephen, ed. *Encountering Evil*. Atlanta: John Knox, 1973.

Dietrich, Donald J. *God and Humanity in Auschwitz: Jewish-Christian Relations and Sanctioned Murder*. New Brunswick, NJ: Transaction, 1995.

Edmonds, Sarah, and Karen Hooker. "Perceived Changes in Life Meaning Following Bereavement." *Omega: Journal of Death and Dying* 25 (4): pp. 307-318 (1992).

Fein, Melvyn. *I.A.M. (Integrated Anger Management): A Common Sense Guide To Coping with Anger*. Westport, CN: Praeger, 1993.

Gassin, Elizabeth A., and Robert D. Enright. "The Will to Meaning in the Process of Forgiveness." *Journal of Psychology and Christianity* 14 (1): pp. 38-49 (1995).

Gaultiere, William J. "A Biblical Perspective on Therapeutic Treatment of Client Anger at God." *Journal of Psychology and Christianity* 8 (3): pp. 38-46 (1989).

Gaultiere, William, and Kristi Gaultiere. *Mistaken Identity*. Old Tappan, NJ: Revell, 1989.

Gerwood, Joseph B. "Meaning and Love in Viktor Frankl's Writing: Reports from the Holocaust." *Psychological Reports* 75 (3): pp. 1075-1081 (1994).

Gladson, Jenny A. "Higher Than the Heavens: Forgiveness in the Old Testament." *Journal of Psychology and Christianity* 11 (2): pp. 125-135 (1992).

Greehy, John J. "Theology Forum: The Cursing Psalms." *The Furrow* 29: pp. 170-174 (1978).

Hass, Aaron. *In the Shadow of the Holocaust: The Second Generation*. Ithaca, NY: Cornell University Press, 1990.

Hick, John. *Evil and the God of Love*. San Francisco: Harper & Row, 1977.

Kane, Donna, Sharon E. Cheston, and Joanne Greer. "Perceptions of God by Survivors of Childhood Sexual Abuse: An Exploratory Study in an Under-researched Area." *Journal of Psychology and Theology* 21 (3): pp. 228-237 (1993).

Kassinove, Howard, ed. *Anger Disorders: Definition, Diagnosis, and Treatment.* Philadelphia: Taylor and Francis, 1995.

Kreeft, Peter. *Making Sense Out of Suffering.* Ann Arbor, MI: Servant, 1986.

Krone, Lynne C. "Justice as a Relational and Theological Cornerstone." *Journal of Psychology and Christianity* 2 (2): pp. 36-46 (1983).

Leavy, Stanley A. *In the Image of God.* New Haven: Yale University Press, 1988.

Leman, Kevin. *Making Children Mind Without Losing Yours.* Grand Rapids, MI: Revell, 2000.

Lerner, Harriet. *The Dance of Anger.* New York: Harper Perennial, 1997.

Lester, Andrew D. "Toward a New Understanding of Anger in Christian Experience." *Review and Expositor* 78: pp. 563-590 (1981).

Lewis, C. S. *A Grief Observed.* New York: Bantam Books, 1961.

Lewis, C. S. *A Severe Mercy.* New York: Bantam Books, 1979.

Lewis, C. S. *God in the Dock: Essays on Theology and Ethics.* Grand Rapids, MI: Eerdmans, 1970.

Lewis, C. S. *Mere Christianity.* New York: Macmillan, 1943.

Lewis, C. S. *The Problem of Pain.* New York: Macmillan, 1962.

Marcus, Paul, and Alan Rosenberg, eds. *Healing Their Wounds: Psychotherapy with Holocaust Survivors and Their Families.* New York: Praeger, 1989.

McQuilkin, Robertson. *A Promise Kept.* Wheaton, IL: Tyndale, 1999.

Mowbray, Thomas L. "The Function in Ministry of Psalms Dealing with Anger: The Angry Psalmist." *The Journal of Pastoral Counseling* 21: pp. 34-39 (1986).

New, David, and Randy Petersen. *How to Fear God Without Being Afraid of Him.* Wheaton, IL: Victor, 1994.

Pedersen, John E. "Some Thoughts on a Biblical View of Anger." *Journal of Psychology and Theology* 2 (3): pp. 210-215 (1974).

Peters, Ted. *Sin: Radical Evil in Soul and Society.* Grand Rapids, MI: Eerdmans, 1994.

Petersen, Randy. "Alone." Drama written for Hope United Methodist Church. Voorhees, NJ, 1997.

Plantinga, Alvin. *God, Freedom, and Evil.* Grand Rapids, MI: Eerdmans, 1974.

Potter-Efron, Ron, and Pat Potter-Efron. *Letting Go of Anger: The 10 Most Common Anger Styles and What to Do About Them.* Oakland, CA: New Harbinger Publications, Inc., 1995.

Rutledge, Aaron L. "Concepts of God Among the Emotionally Upset." *Pastoral Psychology* 2: pp. 22-27 (1951).

Schaeffer, Edith. *Affliction.* Old Tappan, NJ: Revell, 1973.

Silvester, Hugh. *Arguing With God.* Great Britain: InterVarsity, 1977.

Sittser, Gerald. *A Grace Disguised: How the Soul Grows Through Loss.* Grand Rapids, MI: Zondervan, 1996.

Smedes, Lewis. *Forgive and Forget: Healing the Hurts We Don't Deserve.* New York: Pocket Books, 1984.

Smedes, Lewis. *How Can It Be All Right When Everything Is All Wrong?* Great Britain: Harper & Row, 1982.

Smith, R. F., Jr. *Sit Down, God . . . I'm Angry.* Valley Forge, PA: Judson Press, 1997.

Sproul, R. C. *Surprised by Suffering.* Wheaton, IL: Tyndale, 1989.

Stafford, Chase H. "A Biblical Approach to Anger Management Training." *Journal of Psychology and Christianity* 5 (4): pp. 5-11 (1986).

Struck, Jane J. "Forgiving the Dead Man Walking." *Today's Christian Woman* 21 (3): pp. 22-25, 80, 82-86 (1999).

Struck, Jane J. "Funny Girl." *Today's Christian Woman* 20 (6): pp. 52-56, 140-142 (1998).

Talbert, Charles. *Learning Through Suffering.* Collegeville, MN: The Liturgical Press, 1991.

Tashjian, Alice. *Silences.* Princeton, NJ: Blue Pansy Publishing, 1995.

Van De Beek, A. *Why? On Suffering, Guilt, and God.* Grand Rapids, MI: Eerdmans, 1990.

Watson, David. *Fear No Evil.* Wheaton, IL: Tyndale, 1984.

Wenham, John. *The Goodness of God.* Downers Grove, IL: InterVarsity, 1974.

Whiteman, Thomas, and Randy Petersen. *Fresh Start.* Wheaton, IL: Tyndale, 1997.

Willimon, William. *Sighing for Eden: Sin, Evil & the Christian Faith.* Nashville: Abingdon, 1985.

Wolff, Pierre. *Is God Deaf?* Waldwick, NJ: Arena Lettres, 1984.

Wolff, Pierre. *May I Hate God?* New York: Paulist Press, 1979.

Wolterstorff, Nicholas. *Lament for a Son.* Grand Rapids, MI: Eerdmans, 1987.

Woodson, Meg. *Turn It into Glory.* Minneapolis: Bethany, 1991.

Yancey, Philip. *Disappointment with God.* Grand Rapids, MI: Zondervan, 1988.

Yancey, Philip. "When the Facts Don't Add Up." *Christianity Today,* 13 June 1986, pp. 19-22.

NOTES

Chapter One

1. Harriet Lerner, *The Dance of Anger* (New York: Harper Perennial, 1997), p. 1.
2. Sheila Carney, "God Damn God: A Reflection on Expressing Anger in Prayer," *Biblical Theology Bulletin* 13: p. 117 (1983).
3. Carol P. Christ, "Expressing Anger at God," *Anima* 5 (1): p. 4 (1978).
4. Aaron L. Rutledge, "Concepts of God Among the Emotionally Upset," *Pastoral Psychology* 2: p. 23 (1951).
5. William J. Gaultiere, "A Biblical Perspective on Therapeutic Treatment of Client Anger at God," *Journal of Psychology and Christianity* 8 (3): p. 42 (1989).
6. Gaultiere, p. 42.

Chapter Two

1. C. S. Lewis, *Surprised by Joy* (New York: Harcourt Brace, 1955), p. 115.
2. Philip Yancey, *Disappointment with God* (Grand Rapids, MI: Zondervan, 1988).
3. C. S. Lewis, *Mere Christianity* (New York: Macmillan, 1943), p. 45.

Chapter Three

1. Alice Agnes Tashjian, *Silences* (Princeton, NJ: Blue Pansy, 1995), p. 41.
2. Tashjian, p. 41.
3. Tashjian, pp. 41-44.
4. Philip Yancey, *Disappointment with God* (Grand Rapids, MI: Zondervan, 1988), p. 23.
5. C. S. Lewis, *The Problem of Pain* (New York: MacMillan, 1962), p. 40.

6. Lewis, p. 40.
7. William Gaultiere and Kristi Gaultiere, *Mistaken Identity* (Old Tappan, NJ: Revell, 1989), p. 44.
8. Gaultiere and Gaultiere, p. 44.
9. Gaultiere and Gaultiere, p. 53.
10. C. S. Lewis, *God in the Dock* (Grand Rapids, MI: Eerdmans, 1970), pp. 51-52.
11. Lewis, p. 52.
12. Peter Kreeft, *Making Sense Out of Suffering* (Ann Arbor, MI: Servant, 1986), p. 142.

Chapter Four

1. Harriet Lerner, *The Dance of Anger* (New York: Harper Perennial, 1997), pp. 2-3.
2. William J. Gaultiere, "A Biblical Perspective on Therapeutic Treatment of Client Anger at God," *Journal of Psychology and Christianity* 8 (3): p. 38 (1989).
3. B. B. Cunningham, "The Will to Forgive: A Pastoral Theological View of Forgiving," *The Journal of Pastoral Care* 39 (2): p. 141 (1985).
4. Sheila Carney, "God Damn God: A Reflection on Expressing Anger in Prayer," *Biblical Theology Bulletin* 13: p. 118 (1983). Citing H. A. Williams, *Tensions: The Necessary Conflicts in Life and Love* (London: Mitchell Benzley, 1976), pp. 16-17.
5. Carney, p. 118. Citing Carol P. Christ, "Expressing Anger at God," *Anima* 5 (1): p. 7 (1978).
6. Pierre Wolff, *May I Hate God?* (New York: Paulist Press, 1979), pp. 1-2.
7. Carol P. Christ, "Expressing Anger at God," *Anima* 5 (1): pp. 7-8 (1978).
8. Carney, p. 118.
9. Lerner, pp.106-107.

Chapter Five

1. Randy Petersen, "Alone" (drama written for Hope United Methodist Church, Voorhees, NJ), 1997.
2. Viktor Frankl, as cited in Sarah Edmonds and Karen Hooker,

"Perceived Changes in Life Meaning Following Bereavement," *Omega: Journal of Death and Dying* 25 (4), p. 308 (1992).

3. Robertson McQuilkin, *A Promise Kept* (Wheaton, IL: Tyndale, 1999), pp. 10-11.

4. Kevin Leman, *Making Children Mind Without Losing Yours* (Grand Rapids, MI: Revell, 2000).

5. Philip Yancey, "When the Facts Don't Add Up," *Christianity Today*, 13 June 1986, p. 22.

6. C. S. Lewis, *The Problem of Pain* (New York: Macmillan, 1962), p. 115.

Chapter Six

1. J. A. Gladson, "Higher Than the Heavens: Forgiveness in the Old Testament," *Journal of Psychology and Christianity* 11 (2), p. 126 (1992).

2. Elizabeth A. Gassin and Robert D. Enright, "The Will to Meaning in the Process of Forgiveness," *Journal of Psychology and Christianity* 14 (1), pp. 38-39 (1995).

3. Lewis Smedes, *Forgive and Forget* (New York: Pocket Books, 1984), pp. 13-15.

4. Smedes, p. 60.

5. Thomas Whiteman and Randy Petersen, *Fresh Start* (Wheaton, IL: Tyndale, 1997), p. 129.

6. Gladson, p. 126.

7. Smedes, p. 115.

8. Pierre Wolff, *May I Hate God?* (New York: Paulist Press, 1979), p. 57.

Appendix

1. William Gaultiere and Kristi Gaultiere, *Mistaken Identity* (Old Tappan, NJ: Revell, 1989), pp. 20-21.

2. William J. Gaultiere, "A Biblical Perspective on Therapeutic Treatment of Client Anger at God," *Journal of Psychology and Christianity* 8 (3): pp. 38, 40 (1989).

About the Authors

MICHELE NOVOTNI, Ph.D., is an associate professor in the graduate counseling program at Eastern College in St. Davids, Pennsylvania, and a licensed psychologist in private practice. Michele is a frequent speaker at local, state, regional, and national conferences and workshops on faith-based issues related to emotional and psychological growth. She is the coauthor of *Adult ADD* (Piñon Press), *Songs of the Soul* (self-published) and author of *What Does Everybody Else Know That I Don't?* (Specialty Press).

Michele grew up observing her grandmother's anger with God. Her grandmother, Helen Jamgochian, was a survivor of the Armenian Genocide of 1915-1921 in which more than 1.5 million Armenians were killed. Helen saw most of her family killed for their refusal to renounce God and she herself suffered deeply. She struggled with what she saw as the only two explanations for this suffering: either God didn't exist, or he didn't care.

It took eighty years for Michele's grandmother to let go of her anger with God and experience his forgiveness. In one of her final conversations, she told Michele, "I regret that I didn't make peace with God sooner. All I can do now is let you tell others my story so that maybe they won't wait so long." With those words, Michele began her journey writing *Angry with God*.

Michele lives in Malvern, Pennsylvania, with her husband and two sons. Arrangements for Michele to speak to your group or organization can be made by contacting the Wayne Counseling Center, 987 Old Eagle School Road, Suite 719, Wayne, PA, 19087; 610/971-0700.

RANDY PETERSEN has written numerous books, including several on psychological and spiritual themes. He is coauthor of *Stress Test*, *Victim of Love?*, and *Starting Over* (all Piñon Press). Randy regularly creates educational curriculum for youth and adults through Priority One Publications and Mainstay Church Resources. He lives in Westville, New Jersey.

LEARN LOVE AND TRUST OF THE LASTING KIND.

Trusting God

It's easy to trust God when everything's going your way. But how do you keep faith in God when you have a tragic car accident, lose a job, or discover you have cancer? This book will teach you how to trust God completely, even in the face of adversity.

Trusting God (Jerry Bridges) $14

Bold Love

The kind of love modeled by Jesus Christ has nothing to do with manners or unconditional acceptance. Learn to love others in a way that has a significant, life-changing impact on family, friends, coworkers—and even your enemies!

Bold Love (Dan Allender and Tremper Longman III) $16

Get your copies today at your local bookstore, or call (800) 366-7788 and ask for offer **#6135**.